Alternatives in Education: Freedom to Choose

Vernon Smith
Robert Barr
Daniel Burke

ALTERNATIVES IN EDUCATION

Freedom to Choose

By
Vernon Smith,
Robert Barr,
and
Daniel Burke

PHI DELTA KAPPA
Educational Foundation
Bloomington, Indiana

Perspectives in American Education

This book is one of a five-volume set published by Phi Delta Kappa as part of its national bicentennial year program.
The other titles in the set are:

The Purposes of Education, by Stephen K. Bailey
Values in Education, by Max Lerner
Women in Education, by Patricia C. Sexton
Melting of the Ethnics: Education of the Immigrants, 1880–1914, by Mark Krug

Introduction

The two hundredth anniversary of the American declaration of separation from the government of England has stimulated millions of words of sentiment, analysis, nostalgia, and expectation. Much of this verbal and pictorial outpouring has been a kind of patriotic breast-beating. Most of it has been rhetoric.

Several years ago the leadership of Phi Delta Kappa announced its determination to offer a significant contribution to the bicentennial celebration in a series of authoritative statements about major facets of American education that would deserve the attention of serious scholars in education, serve the needs of neophytes in the profession, and survive as an important permanent contribution to the educational literature.

The Board of Directors and staff of Phi Delta Kappa, the Board of Governors of the Phi Delta Kappa Educational Foundation, and the Project '76 Implementation Committee all made important contributions to the creation of the Bicentennial Activities Program, of which this set of books is only one of seven notable projects. The entire program has been made possible by the loyal contributions of dedicated Kappans who volunteered as Minutemen, Patriots, and Bell Ringers according to the size of their donations and by the support of the Educational Foundation, based on the generous bequest of George Reavis. The purpose of the Foundation, as stated at its inception, is to contribute to a better understanding of the educative process and the relation of education to human welfare. These five volumes should serve that purpose well.

A number of persons should be recognized for their

contributions to the success of this enterprise. The Board of Governors of the Foundation, under the leadership of Gordon Swanson, persevered in the early planning stages to insure that the effort would be made. Other members of the board during this period were Edgar Dale, Bessie Gabbard, Arliss Roaden, Howard Soule, Bill Turney, and Ted Gordon, now deceased.

The Project '76 Implementation Committee, which wrestled successfully with the myriad details of planning, financing, and publicizing the seven activities, included David Clark, Jack Frymier, James Walden, Forbis Jordan, and Ted Gordon.

The Board of Directors of Phi Delta Kappa, 1976 to 1978, include President Bill L. Turney, President-Elect Gerald Leischuck, Vice Presidents William K. Poston, Rex K. Reckewey, and Ray Tobiason and District Representatives Gerald L. Berry, Jerome G. Kopp, James York, Cecil K. Phillips, Don Park, Philip G. Meissner, and Carrel Anderson.

The major contributors to this set of five perspectives on American education are of course the authors. They have found time in busy professional schedules to produce substantial and memorable manuscripts, both scholarly and readable. They have things to say about education that are worth saying, and they have said them well. They have made a genuine contribution to the literature, helping to make a fitting contribution to the celebration of two hundred years of national freedom. More importantly, they have articulated ideas so basic to the maintenance of that freedom that they should be read and heeded as valued guidelines for the years ahead, hopefully at least another two hundred.

—Lowell Rose
Executive Secretary,
Phi Delta Kappa

Contents

Preface

Today it is fashionable to be critical of public education. In 1970 we were very fashionable. We were also discouraged about the failure of efforts to change the schools and pessimistic about the future of education and the future of society. We feel differently today. While we are by no means euphoric, we are confident that the means to improve the schools are at hand. Whether communities will take advantage of these means and develop school systems consistent with a democratic society and appropriate for the world of the future is an open question. This book makes no attempt to answer that question. Nor does this book advocate alternative schools in every community. What it does suggest is that every community needs to consider the role of the schools in the future of its youth. We hope this book will contribute to such consideration.

Acknowledgment

In the more than five years that the three of us have been working together with the development of optional public schools, we have received much help and support and many suggestions, including a few very blunt ones, from a host of concerned people. It would be impossible to acknowledge them all here. But we do wish to acknowledge a few people who have worked closely with us through these years: David Clark of Indiana University, Mario Fantini of the New York State University College at New Paltz, Nate Blackman of the Chicago Public Schools, Ginna Brock of the California State Department of Education, Barbara Case of the Tulsa Public Schools, Alf Clinton of the Vancouver, British Columbia, Public Schools, Martha Ellison of the Louisville Public Schools, Mike Hickey of the Seattle Public Schools, Bill Howell of the Columbia, South Carolina, Public Schools, Jim Jenkins of the Orange County, California, Public Schools, Wayne Jennings of the St. Paul Public Schools, Jim Moore of the Florida State Department of Education, John Newton of the Berkeley Public Schools, Dolores Paskal of the Wayne County, Michigan, Intermediate School District, Leslie Paffrath of the Johnson Foundation, Don Robinson of Phi Delta Kappa, Ray Shurtleff of the Cambridge Public Schools, the late John Stanavage of the North Central Association, Bob Stark of the Grand Rapids Public Schools, and Betty Jo Zander of the Minneapolis Public Schools. We thank you all.

We are especially grateful for the opportunity to discuss our ideas on alternatives with people who were involved in four recent national reports on education and the need for school reform: B. Frank Brown, director, Information and Services Program of the Institute for Development of Educational Activities and chairman of the National Commission on the Reform of Secondary Education and Director of Task Force '74; James S. Coleman, professor of sociology, University of Chicago, and chairman, Panel on Youth of the President's Science Advisory Committee; and John Henry Martin, executive vice president, Initial Teaching Alphabet Foundation, and chairman, National Panel on High Schools and Adolescent Education of the U.S. Office of Education. Their reactions and suggestions were most helpful.

Above all we wish to thank the many students, teachers, and parents who have shown us that optional public schools work.

Vernon H. Smith
Robert D. Barr
Daniel J. Burke
Indiana University

The Role of Alternatives in Education

A Historical Perspective

Alternatives have always existed in American education. The diversity and availability of alternatives have varied with time and location, with social, political, and economic conditions, and with race, religion, and other cultural factors. But, in general, as the country expanded and developed from colonial times to modern, educational alternatives have diminished. For children and youth growing up in the third quarter of the twentieth century fewer options in education were available than in any earlier period in America's 200-year history.

The present pattern of public education, with more than 90 percent of the population between ages five and seventeen assigned to a specific public school and required by law to attend it, is a recent development. Choices about education that were basically the prerogative of the family for more than 200 years (1642–1852) have all but disappeared for the overwhelming majority of American families today. No one in colonial times, including the founding fathers, could have predicted or envisioned the present system of universal compulsory public education.

Lawrence A. Cremin in *American Education: The Colonial Experience* described educational alternatives of the colonial period (1607–1783):

By the middle of the eighteenth century, the educational institutions of provincial America constituted a fascinating kaleidoscope of endless diversity and change. . . . Furthermore, given the continued novelty and unprecedented opportunity of the provincial situation, all these institutions, each in its own way, found themselves wrestling in their day-to-day operation with insistent problems of stability and change. Parents were inevitably caught in heartrending dilemmas as to whether to hold their offspring to older ways or encourage them along newer lines. . . .

It is difficult to generalize with any degree of precision about the extent of schooling in provincial America, largely because of the phenomenal variation in types and modes of instruction and the consequent difficulty of determining exactly what to call a school. . . .

The combinations and permutations were legion, and the larger and more heterogenous the community, the greater the latitude and diversity of the arrangements [of schools]. . . .

. . . [W]ith the proliferation of types of schooling, the concomitant increase in the variety of printed textual materials for instruction and self-instruction, and the development of libraries for the collection and dissemination of such materials, the range of possible life-styles open to a given individual beyond the particular version proferred by his family, his church, or even his neighboring school or surrounding community, was vastly enlarged. A particular school might or might not have been liberating for a particular individual; but the institution of schooling in general, when coupled with the flow of didactic material from the press, was indeed liberating, in that it provided genuine life alternatives. . . .

Thus Cremin reports diversity, family choice, a "phenomenal variation in types and modes of instruction," and "the proliferation of types of schooling" in prerevolutionary America. Cremin and others have documented a surprising diversity of schooling that was available, particularly in the cities and large communities. By 1800 three general types of schools were available in the well populated areas: the English or common school, the Latin grammar school, and the academy. Parochial schools were common, including Anglican, Catholic, Huguenot, Lutheran, Presbyterian, and Quaker schools. Evening schools were available in some communities to meet the needs of children and youth who worked in the daytime. A wide variation appeared among colleges, particularly after the Revolution, and the distinctions between colleges and the lower schools were blurred.

Cremin also reported the availability of individual teachers in "reading, writing, ciphering, grammar, bookkeeping, surveying, navigation, fencing, dancing, music, modern languages, embroidery, and every conceivable combination of these and other subjects."

In spite of the diversity of schools, schooling was relatively unimportant to the average citizen in colonial America. The majority of American adults at the time of the Revolution had never attended school. Most of those who had, had attended for only a year or two. While society ranked education as paramount, it gave the schools a minor role. Schooling was only one of the educational alternatives and was far from the most important one. As an educational agency of society, the school ranked last after 1) the family and home, 2) the neighborhood and local community, and 3) work, either on the family farm, in the family business, or in an apprenticeship arranged by parents for their children. For the few who were members of established churches, religion also outranked school in its importance as an educational agency. Many small communities lacked schools of any kind. In larger communities where schools were available, only a minority of those of school age attended. Schooling, even for elementary grades, did not begin to be compulsory until the last half of the nineteenth century.

Where schools existed, the school "year" was short, usually only a few weeks. The majority of children were expected to attend for only a few years. When work needed to be done at home or other responsibilities appeared within the community, children were expected to forego school. Even for the children involved, school must have been a relatively insignificant event, except for the social contacts with others in their general age group.

Therefore, the routine expectation of typical colonial parents was that a variety of schools would be available at varying prices for their children if they chose to send their children to school at all.

Education and schooling are not mentioned in the U.S. Constitution, ratified in 1789. In *The Public School Movement* Richard Pratte suggests that this was either because the idea of free public schools or a federal school system had not occurred to the founding fathers or that they thought the issue would be too controversial. It is also possible that schooling just wasn't very important to the majority of those who were framing the Constitution.

Thomas Jefferson did consider school important. He was a proponent of mass education, and he envisioned the "schooled" electorate as a necessity for a democratic nation. Jefferson did not participate in the constitutional convention, and he wanted an amendment to the Constitution to aid public education. In 1779 he sponsored an unsuccessful bill in the Virginia legislature that would have provided three years of schooling without charge for each free child in the state. Thirty-five years later, in 1814, he proposed a similar bill, which was also defeated. Other Virginia legislators did not share his enthusiasm for public education. Neither of Jefferson's bills suggested compulsory schooling. He probably assumed that most, if not all, families would take advantage of the opportunity.

In his lifetime he was unable to convince Virginians of the importance of his modest aspirations for a school in every community and three years of free public schooling for every child. He never advocated compulsory schooling because he was reluctant to oppose the will of the parents.

It is likely that Jefferson's libertarian thinking was somewhat akin to that expressed half a century later by John Stuart Mill, who in his famous essay *On Liberty* in 1859 warned against state-controlled schooling in a democratic society.

> All that has been said of the importance of individuality of character, and diversity in opinions and modes of conduct, involves, as of the same unspeakable importance, diversity of education. A general state education is a mere contrivance for molding people to be exactly like one another. And as the mold in which it casts them is that which pleases the predominant power in the government, whether this be a monarch, a priesthood, an aristocracy, or the majority of the existing generation in proportion as it is efficient and successful, it establishes a despotism over the mind, leading by natural tendency to one over the body. An education established and controlled by the state should only exist, if it exist at all, as one among many competing experiments, carried on for the purpose of example and stimulus, to keep the others up to a certain standard of excellence.

By today's standards Jefferson was an elitist, believing that only a small number of youth needed schooling beyond grammar school, including those whose families could afford private education and those who were of unusual academic ability and whose further schooling would therefore be supported by the state.

No one in Jefferson's time could have foreseen today's bureaucratic system of public schooling in which students are assigned to schools and compelled to attend them for a major portion of their first twenty years of life. While early laws in New England made parents responsible for the literacy of their children and made communities of a certain minimum size responsible for providing a common school, the concept of compulsory attendance was not even considered.

The recording of the history of education creates its own mythology. Those who were best educated are likely to have kept the best records of their education. Historical bench marks, such as the Massachusetts law of 1642 that made parents responsible for the literacy of their children and the 1647 act that required every town of 100 families or more to provide a school, create the illusion of a well-schooled colonial society. While these Massachusetts laws were initiated for religious reasons, fewer than 10 percent of the total colonial population belonged to established churches. Apparently these laws did not produce universal education, because 200 years later, in 1852, Massachusetts became the first state to pass a compulsory attendance law requiring all children from eight to fourteen to attend school for twelve weeks a year including six consecutive weeks. In *The Transformation of The School* Lawrence Cremin points out that "passing a law does not necessarily get children to school."

By 1860 the concept of universal elementary education was accepted. The majority of states had established public elementary schools, and at least half of the school-age children were attending elementary schools, with the majority in public schools. Attendance at this time was still a family choice, not yet a result of the few state compulsory attendance laws.

By 1900 more than half the states had compulsory attendance laws, and universal compulsory elementary schooling was assured. Also by this time strong criticisms of public schools existed, and numerous experimental schools, both public and nonpublic, were being tried. The Commissioner of Education reported that students attended school on an average of 86 days in 1893–94, leaving adequate time for other educational alternatives.

In the secondary school the situation was markedly different. Throughout the nineteenth century, youth had the option of full-time employment. Public high schools were available for only a small minority. Apprenticeships, on-the-job training, and private schools of various types were frequent choices, but for most youth the family expectation was full-time employment by age twelve to fourteen. Interest in secondary education increased in some states following the establishment of the first public high school in 1821 and became general after the 1872 Kalamazoo Case affirmed the legality of tax-supported secondary schools. But by 1890 this option was still available to only a few. About 7 percent of the fourteen- to seventeen-year-olds were enrolled in secondary schools, and a majority were in public schools for the first time. By 1900 more than 10 percent of this age group were attending, but only a minority of those attending were graduating. Secondary education, public and private, was designed only for the few who were academically successful in the elementary school and who would, if successful in the secondary school, continue on to college. Admission to most large academic secondary schools, public and private, was by examination until about 1920.

The first vocational high school started in St. Louis in 1881, providing an alternative to the academic and a replacement for the apprenticeship, which was no longer widely available. With the general acceptance of vocational education and with the dropping of entrance examinations for secondary schools, the high schools became accessible to more students. Although it is difficult even today to find accurate statistics on enrollment and graduation, it appears that in 1910 about one of four students was enrolled in secondary school, and as many as 10 percent of the total school-age population may have been graduating.

Universal compulsory secondary education, or mass secondary education, was firmly established by 1940, with a majority of the fourteen- to seventeen-year-old population enrolled in high school and with nearly 40 percent graduating. Today mass secondary education is a reality, with almost 90 percent of the age group enrolled and with about 70 percent graduating.

Two conclusions are obvious: First, in America's

200-year history, what was originally a diverse array of educational options has been reduced to one monolithic public school system without choice for the individual family. In addition, the major concern during this period has been on quantity rather than quality. The tremendous effort and expense of providing free public elementary and secondary education for rapidly increasing enrollments has blotted out other concerns. Francis Keppel, former U.S. Commissioner of Education, has predicted the quest for quality and equality will be the coming revolution in American education. For the first time in history Americans are not faced with burgeoning school enrollments.

"Better Than Ever" Is Not Good Enough

Regardless of diminishing educational alternatives, and in spite of the shift from voluntarism to compulsion by a tax-supported bureaucracy, public school systems that evolved during 200 years have accomplished a monumental task. American public schools are the best in the world. A larger proportion of children and youth go to school and go farther in school than in any other country, ancient or modern. Further, this has been accomplished with a heterogenous population, with large numbers of non-English speaking immigrants, and with rapidly increasing enrollments. Even to solve the logistic problems of schooling for more than 50 million students, or almost one-fourth of the population, is an amazing feat.

Today's schools are better than ever. Adequate evidence based on achievement tests and other measures shows that today's children learn more in school than their parents or grandparents did, both in basic skills and in other curricular areas. This is not to state that today's schools are either "good" or effective. In the last two decades society's expectations for schools have far exceeded the capacity of schools to respond to these expectations—universal literacy, mass elementary and secondary education, racial and social integration, equality of educational opportunity, and higher education for those who desire it. Schools cannot respond adequately to these twentieth-century expectations earlier than the twenty-first century.

More than one million students have dropped out before graduating from high school each year since 1960, and this trend is projected to continue through 1980. These dropouts are from all levels of ability and all socioeconomic levels. The national dropout rate is more than 25 percent and may be as high as 40 percent. When school enrollments were increasing in the 1950s and 1960s, the dropout rate was declining, leading some to believe that time would solve the problem. Today, with declining enrollments in the schools, the dropout rate is on the way up. A Senate committee reported that the dropout rate increased 11.7 percent between 1970 and 1973. California reports a 50 percent increase of dropouts since 1970. Shelley Umans says in *How To Cut the Cost of Education,* "Forty percent of all high school students drop out before graduation." More than half of the total adult population have not completed high school.

Many other students in each high school graduating class have stayed in school but have not benefited significantly from their twelve-year investment. One evidence of this is alarmingly high absence and truancy rates in urban areas. Surveys among the members of the National Association of Secondary School Principals have shown that absenteeism is ranked as the number one problem, far ahead of discipline, which is number two. Figures on absenteeism in individual schools and school districts vary widely. Walberg and Sigler report in the May, 1975, *Phi Delta Kappan,* "One school reporting 90 percent daily attendance has as few as 20 percent of the students on class lists actually in their classes."

"We have looked away so long from the poor child going to school that even in this heralded moment of enormous technological capacity, we have only the

slightest notion of how many poor children are in
school," Thomas Cottle wrote in 1974. "Our census
data are wholly inadequate; the actual estimates of
children out of school run into millions."

Estimates on the number of school-age children and
youth not enrolled in school vary from a low of two
million to a high of ten million. A report by the
Children's Defense Fund in 1974 indicates that the
two million out-of-school children reported by the U.S.
Census are only a fraction of the total number.

The Children's Defense Fund found in studying
suspensions that one of every 24 students in school
districts reporting was suspended in the 1972–73
school year. In the secondary school the figure was
one out of thirteen. More than 60 percent of these
suspensions were for nondangerous, nonviolent offenses, fewer than 3 percent for "destruction of
property, criminal activity, or use of drugs or alcohol."

For more than a decade some people have recognized
that the schools are not responding effectively to the
needs of the poor and the culturally different, but
anyone who goes to an all-white, middle-class, suburban school will see some children or youth who are
not succeeding. At the 1975 NEA Conference on
Educational Neglect, William Rohwer reported that
nearly 33 percent of white students from middle-class
families and almost 45 percent of black students from
poor families fail to receive grades of C or better.

More than one million youth ages 12 to 17 cannot
read at the beginning fourth-grade level. A 1975 Office
of Education study indicates that more than half of
American adults are either incompetent or barely
competent in the minimal skills necessary for survival
in contemporary society.

A national study in 1968 reported that little thought-
ful attention had been given to the English curriculum
for the middle 50 percent in the high schools and
predicted that years would pass before effective programs for the large group in the middle were devel-

oped. Recently, the Organization of American His-
torians warned that the teaching of American history
in the public schools was "in crisis." The National
Assessment of Educational Progress reported in 1975
that the majority of 17-year-olds and young adults
were incompetent in solving everyday consumer problems in mathematics and that science test scores had
declined since 1972.

A U.S. Office of Education report in 1970 stated
that those most neglected in the schools were the gifted.
A growing body of informed opinion asserts that the
major causes of today's school deficiencies are the
failure to adapt the school to changing conditions and
the failure to provide alternatives.

In 1967 John Goodlad suggested, "The incidence
of nonpromotion, dropouts, alienation, and minimal
learning in school is such that one is led to conclude
that today's schools are obsolescent."

Congressman William Steiger of Wisconsin, in a
speech at a conference on American Youth in the
Mid-Seventies, said: "Every year, 2.5 million young
people drop out of high school, graduate from a
'general curriculum,' or drop out of college without
completing a degree program. Our society has regarded
this group as the 'failures,' for they have not 'completed' the educational stream we have developed for them;
we now realize that we have failed in not providing
meaningful alternatives to the college preparatory
course."

In the report of a 1973 national conference, *The
Greening of the High School,* appears the assertion,
"This, then is the condition that confronts us:
though youth is no longer the same, and the world
is no longer the same, high schools are essentially
unchanged from what they were at the beginning of
the century."

A 1974 publication, *Developing New Models, Methods, and Means for Education* by the Institute for
the Development of Education Activities, reports:

"American schools apparently were designed for a different culture, a different concept of learning and teaching, and a different clientele than they now serve."

It is not necessary to review the recent reports on vandalism, violence, and crime in the schools. Should taxpayers be spending more for vandalism in the schools than for textbooks—more than $500 million annually?

The conclusion that "better schools than ever before" are not good enough will disturb some readers. After more than two decades of sincere attempts to reform public education, it is difficult to accept the conclusion that schools are not effectively responding to the living and learning needs of the majority of their clientele.

Nevertheless, this conclusion is both valid and well verified. At least a dozen national reports on schools published since 1970 suggest that schools are in a state of crisis and that drastic reforms are called for. But more importantly, these recent national reports endorse the need for alternatives in public education.

Why Alternatives in Education?

In a democratic society people should have choices in all important aspects of their lives. The present monolithic structure for public education, in which all children and youth are assigned without choice to a public school, evolved more by accident than by intent. Students, their families, teachers, and other educators would benefit if they had choice from a plurality of alternatives within public school systems. In *The Soft Revolution* Neil Postman and Charles Weingartner wrote, "A major characteristic of the American culture is that it is pluralistic. If pluralism means anything, it means the availability of options. Where there are no options, you have a fraudulent pluralism—the name without the reality. This is true in business, as well as in government. It is also true in education.

"At present, our educational system is monolithic. One has no choice but to accept the sole approach to learning offered by the schools. The situation, if not un-American, is not American in spirit."

Who Decides?

People closest to the action should have the largest share in deciding what goes on in a school. The local community, the families involved, and the professional staff should all share in decisions that affect their lives. People prefer to make real choices among real alternatives.

The Task Force '74 report, *The Adolescent, Other Citizens, and Their High Schools,* states: "Gradually, the institution of education has moved away from the basic premise of democracy: that people should control their institutions. Education is the public institution closest to the people. Citizens have the right to be involved in governance, policy making, and decisions affecting schools."

An informed and educated electorate is needed to make wise decisions about the future course of a democratic society. The best preparation for decision making is making decisions. To have adults who will make wise decisions tomorrow, students must have opportunities for decision making today. One way to accomplish this is to provide alternatives in education and let students and their families choose from these alternatives.

Learning and Alternatives

"In a society as diverse and complex as ours, no institution can effectively serve all people," says Owen Kiernan, executive secretary of the National Association of Secondary School Principals. "By the same token, schools should not be judged as failures if all students do not meet with immediate academic and life-related success. Most students respond well to what educators have come to describe as the traditional approach, while others require alternatives in nontraditional categories. The fact that we continue to have almost one million high school dropouts each year gives credence to the fact that the standard offerings simply do not meet the needs of all students."

If educators accept that different people learn in different ways and at different times, what sense does it make to assign all of the eight-year-olds in one neighborhood to one school and to one classroom within that school?

When James B. Conant wrote *The American High School Today* in 1959, he was concerned about the effectiveness of the comprehensive high school in meeting the needs of the academically talented, a group he described as the top 15 percent in scholastic aptitude. He suggested that some "in the next lower 10 to 20 percent" could benefit from similar but less rigorous academic programs. But American high schools had always been designed for the academically talented. Possibly because Conant's report was the only one at the time, or possibly because Americans were very much concerned about the space race then, his report evoked much praise and little criticism. It is gratifying to be told to continue to do a little better what you've been doing all the time.

In 1960 the Bruner report, *The Process of Education*, also emphasized cognitive or academic learning, and Americans embarked on a decade of reforms to improve the curriculum for the academically talented, a minority of 15 to 20 percent of the population according to Conant's figures. Because the majority of children and youth are not academically talented, the majority are being deprived of equal educational opportunity when they are assigned without choice to the standard public school.

In addition to concern for the talented, concern is increasing about the failure of schools to develop the basic skills. "Students themselves are not the causes of reading failure," say Ronald Santora and Louise Jensen. "While some of the causes of reading failure are surely psychological, reading failure is not caused by children who have been labeled as 'defective' in some cognitive sense or as 'deficient' in some linguistic sense. If failure has occurred, it is most often the failure of the schools themselves, their environments, attitudes, and methods of instruction (or all three). It is the schools that must attempt to restructure themselves in order to accommodate a linguistic and cultural pluralism among those they serve. If this sounds like a plea for alternative learning environments, it is."

This suggests that the failure to provide alternative learning environments deprives some children and youth of equal educational opportunity. Assigning all children in the community to one school forces students to "fit" the school. Providing alternative schools or environments creates opportunities for making schools fit the students.

Blending Education and Life

The 1974 Coleman report, *Youth: Transition to Adulthood,* begins with these lines:

> As the labor of children has become unnecessary to society, school has been extended for them. With every decade, the length of schooling has increased, until a thoughtful person must ask whether society can conceive of no other way for youth to come into adulthood. If schooling were a complete environment, the answer would properly be that no amount of school is too much, and increased schooling for the young is the best way for the young to spend their increased leisure, and society its increased wealth.
>
> But schooling, as we know it, is not a complete environment giving all the necessary opportunities for becoming adult. School is a certain kind of environment: individualistic, oriented toward cognitive achievement, imposing dependency on and withholding authority and responsibility from those in the role of students. So long as school was short and merely a supplement to the main activities of growing up, this mattered little.

Education cannot be divorced from the realities of life. Learning in school should not be isolated from the world outside the school. The report quoted above and three other national reports on the schools published between 1973 and 1975 are unanimous in their criticism of schools for isolating youth from society and for segregating youth from adults and from other age groups in schools. These reports recommend developing educational alternatives to provide action learning, community service, and career awareness, and to promote social responsibility. In spite of the consensus among these reports, some firmly believe that the school's role should be oriented toward cognitive achievement and that the development of social responsibility is not the role of the schools, but should become, as it was in colonial days, the responsibility of home, church, and community.

Cultural Pluralism vs. Public Schooling

In 1971 the Supreme Court abolished compulsory education beyond the elementary school for the Amish. The Court's opinion said, in part, "The high school tends to emphasize intellectual and scientific accomplishments, self-distinction, competitiveness, worldly success, and social life with other students. Amish society emphasizes informal learning through doing; a life of 'goodness' rather than a life of intellect; wisdom, rather than technical knowledge; community welfare, rather than competition; and separation from, rather than integration with, contemporary worldly society."

Other parents might also prefer wisdom and cooperation to self-distinction and competition for their children. As a nation Americans have taken pride in cultural pluralism, but the schools have never reflected that pride. The schools' assigned responsibility for Americanizing children of immigrants was interpreted as homogenizing children of all racial and ethnic groups. The failure of schools to be effective for and responsive to children of minority groups is well documented. When all the children from diverse groups within the culture were assigned to one school, it was natural for the school to expect them to conform. Today people are more aware of the problems of conflicting value systems, racial prejudice and fear, and the various educational expectations of different cultural groups. But the standard school has not adjusted to the legitimate demands of a pluralistic society, and recent developments in public education suggest that schools are becoming less able to meet the needs of a pluralistic society. "A plea for pluralism may be in conflict with much that is happening in contemporary American education: increasing consolidation and centralization, national assessment programs, curriculum projects prepared by outside experts, performance or behavioral objectives for children, and demands for stricter accountability of educators' performances by public officials," says Clinton Allison in *Without Consensus: Issues in American Education.* "Although often unintended, all of these have the effect, unless those responsible for their implementation are extremely careful, of further standardizing the schools. If education is to reflect the pluralistic nature of our society, our need is not for more standardization, but for an opening of possibilities for experimentation with ways of teaching, learning, and living. Consensus on issues in American education is neither needed nor desirable."

The Public Image of Public Education

Schooling is more important today than at any previous time in American history for two reasons: First, children and youth are spending so much more time in schools that school has become the major institution in their development into adults in society. A second reason is that the cost of this universal elementary and secondary education is one of the major expenses of society. As a result, educators and education are part of the power struggle within the national economy.

During the decade 1960 to 1970, expenditures for public education rose at a much faster rate than the national economy or the Gross National Product. The natural result of education getting a larger share of available money was the call for accountability from sectors that received smaller shares. Educators have not yet fully perceived the influence that this changing power structure will have on the future of public education.

To further complicate this power struggle within the national economy, the public image of the schools is at an ebb. Today people are much more sophisticated in analyzing problems than in solving them. The critics of the schools are better at disparaging than the educators are at improving. The media make the schools' shortcomings, both real and imagined, general knowledge. Educators will have to compete for funds in the unfamiliar national arena with a weakened public image of the schools.

All alternatives that may contribute to more responsive systems of public education and that may strengthen American education as a whole must be examined. The North Central Association's *Policies and Standards for the Accreditation of Optional Schools* begins with these lines: "In recent years the concept of educational choice (optional schools, alternative schools—call them what you will) has penetrated deeply in the American system of education. It seems likely that in the foreseeable future many different types of schools will exist side by side within the total educational structure, each designed to meet a different set of specified learning and living needs of young people. These schools will not be competitive with nor antagonistic to one another, but rather will be complementary in effort and thrust, helping American education redeem its long-term commitment to the fullest education of every child."

Tomorrow's Schools Today

"Every society must somehow solve the problem of transforming children into adults, for its very survival depends on that solution," said James Coleman in *Youth: Transition to Adulthood.* In a similar vein, Alvin Toffler said in *Future Shock,* "Just as genetic diversity favors the survival of species, educational diversity increases the odds for survival of societies."

Futurists seem to agree on a general strategy for planning—to design or describe possible alternative futures, to determine which are most probable and most desirable, and to start moving now toward the more desirable. Planning in education could be a simple matter. Any school or other learning experience that can be designed today can be tried today as one choice among others.

Possible alternative schools and options to schooling need to be examined to select those that are most desirable within a community and to make them available by choice within that community. Today's alternatives are the laboratories for tomorrow's education.

John Gardner, former U.S. Commissioner of Education, said in 1970, "I think the pieces of an educational revolution are lying around unassembled, and I think we're going to put them together in the next few years." A move from compulsion to choice in schooling must appear before the framework for the revolution will be built.

The future is everybody's business. It is too fragile and uncertain to trust to an elite few. Children and youth must be educated for the parts they will play in determining the future of all. In commenting on the role of youth, Toffler says, "The rest of us need all the energy, brains, imagination, and talent that young people can bring to bear on our difficulties. For the society to attempt to solve its desperate problems without the full participation of even very young people is imbecile."

What Are the Alternatives?

M any developments in the past two decades, such as consolidation of school districts, construction of larger school buildings, intervention by federal and state governments, and development of new curricula nationally, have operated to standardize public schools. The creation of alternative public schools is, in part, a reaction against standardization, because alternative schools would diversify educational opportunities within a community.

While alternatives have always existed in American education, in this century alternative schools have not been accessible to the majority of families. From 1940 to the present, alternatives have been available to a smaller proportion of the citizenry than in any earlier period. There have always been private schools for families who could afford them and parochial schools for families who preferred them. Until after 1850 more children and youth were enrolled in nonpublic schools than in public schools. By 1970 the enrollment in nonpublic schools had dropped below 10 percent of total elementary and secondary school enrollment for the first time, and this decline in nonpublic school enrollment is projected to continue at least through 1980. Thus more than 90 percent of America's children will attend public schools in the forseeable future. If alternatives are desirable for some students, they will have to be provided within public school systems, for that is where the students are. Few families can afford the luxury of the private school.

By 1970 interest in educational alternatives within public school systems began to increase. Many reasons have been cited for this increase. The most acceptable is this: After reform attempts in the 1960s, some educators realized that the quest for a perfect school that would meet the needs of all students had failed. They began to question the assumption that a single school or program could serve the learning needs of all children or youth. One obvious solution was exploring alternatives. This new approach to change, the provision of optional alternatives within public school systems, began to appear in professional literature and to be reflected in national reports. The 1970 White House Conference on Children recommended "immediate, massive funding for the development of alternative optional forms of public education." By 1975 more than a dozen national reports had recommended the development of alternatives within public school systems.

The opening of the Parkway Program in Philadelphia in 1969 caught the attention of the media, and Parkway became the symbol of the alternative public school movement. Reports on Parkway appeared on national television, in professional and popular periodicals, and in Sunday supplements of newspapers throughout the country. Although successful alternative public schools were in operation long before this, Parkway was the first alternative public school designed to be available by option to any high school student in its community, the city of Philadelphia, and the first designed to use the community as a learning environment. In practice this program proved so popular that the administration was unequipped to expand it fast enough to accommodate all the eager applicants, so students were selected for admission by a lottery system. Parkway has had several thousand visitors each year, including parents, teachers, and administrators from all parts of the country and from many other countries. Several other communities have since developed their own schools without walls following the Parkway form.

With a well-publicized model like Parkway and with strong recommendations in major national reports, it would be reasonable to expect the concept of alternative public schools to have been well accepted and implemented in many communities by now. To date, this has not occurred. While more than 5,000 alternative public schools are in operation today, their total enrollment is probably about one million, or approximately 2 percent of the total elementary and secondary school enrollment. Only a small proportion of families, perhaps as many as 10 percent, have a choice of alternative public schools within their communities. About one-fourth of the more than 15,000 school systems in America may be providing some form of alternative education for students within the community. Only a handful of communities, including Berkeley, Grand Rapids, and Minneapolis, are moving to options for every family.

Resistance to Alternative Programs

While public and professional interest in alternative schools and programs seems to be increasing, at the same time several factors are inhibiting their adoption. The concept of optional alternative public schools is not well accepted by the mainstream of society or of educators. A general stigma on the alternative school can be expressed: "Alternative schools are for someone else's children." The reasons for this stigma and for the related resistance to alternatives in many communities are complex.

Part of the problem results from factors beyond the public schools. A. S. Neill, the founder of Summerhill, a small, private residential school in England, has had a wide audience in this country. Neill's philosophy, originally stated in 1960 in *Summerhill,* that letting children do what they want will eventually result in effective learning, has not been widely ac-

cepted here. But Neill's Summerhill became a model
for many nonpublic free schools that opened in the
late '60s. These schools, sometimes called alternative
schools, became associated in the minds of many with
the counter-culture, a movement which also made
common use of the word alternative—alternative life-
styles, alternative communities, alternative programs.

After World War II, criticism of public schools
became a new vocation. The media made critics readily
available to the public. Some—Paul Goodman, Jonathan Kozol, George Leonard—extolled the nonpublic
alternative school, thus eliciting antagonism from
public school educators. The politics and rhetoric of
critics and of free schools have tended to solidify
resistance to alternatives in some communities.

Within public school systems are even more barriers
to the development of optional public schools. Although the commonly stated purpose of the public
alternative school is to complement the conventional
school and provide a total system that is responsive
to the needs of more students, many educators perceive
the alternative school as a competitor. In communities
where enrollments are declining for the first time in
history, the alternative school may be viewed as an
adversary in competition for students. Where school
budgets are tight, alternative schools may be viewed
as adversaries in competition for funds.

A stigma is attached to alternative schools in some
areas because the first alternative school in the community was a school for those who were the rejected—
the dropout, the potential dropout, the pregnant, or
the disruptive.

Another barrier to the acceptance of the alternative
school concept is that many communities cling to the
perfect school idea, believing that one school can be
developed to satisfy the learning needs of all students.
For example, when one district built a new open
elementary school, parents on one side of a central
street were told that their children would have to attend

the new open school. Parents on the other side were told that their children would have to attend the older conventional school. Some parents on both sides of the street were furious. If the open school turned out to be the perfect school, it would still be impossible in some communities to force all families to send their children to it.

Confusion About Classifications

Today it is difficult to classify alternatives. Most alternative schools and programs are developed within a community to satisfy a perceived educational need. Terminology is confusing because an alternative school in one community might be the conventional school in another community. An open school in one school district could be quite different from an open school in another. No other area of education seems as cluttered with confusing and emotion-provoking terminology.

Recently some large school districts have created special schools for disruptive students from other schools within the district who are transferred or assigned without choice. These are improperly called alternative schools, because no pupil choice is associated with them.

Another trend has been the shift in some communities from the conventional school to something else. One example is converting all elementary schools to open education. Automatically then, all children in the community are assigned to the open school just as they were formerly assigned to the conventional school. Again, this may be desirable, but it is not the same as the availability of alternatives with clientele determined by choice rather than by compulsion.

Alternatives Within Public School Systems

In summary, much confusion arises about the semantics of alternative schools. What follows is an attempt to clarify the terminology.

Alternatives Within the Standard School

As mentioned earlier, the present system of public
education provides little, if any, choice for the bulk
of students who attend. While it is possible for a family
to select a specific school by choosing a residence
within that school's geographic boundaries, few families can afford this means of choice.

Differentiated Programs. Comprehensive high
schools provide programs or tracks to meet needs of
students. Three programs normally provided are the
academic or college preparatory program, the vocational-technical program, and the general program. It
is difficult to determine how much choice operates
in this system. Whether students and their families
choose programs or whether they are guided into them
without choice is difficult to assess.

Open Enrollment. Some school districts allow students and their parents to select any school within
the system as long as space is available. This arrangement can provide alternatives if schools within the
district have different offerings. In East Lansing,
Michigan, the school board made all elementary
schools available on an open enrollment plan and
encouraged each school staff to develop its own program.

Selection of Teachers. In some school districts students and their parents are permitted to select teachers
within the school. While this is more common in
elementary schools, selection of courses in the secondary schools also gives students some choice of
teachers. Team teaching programs may also allow
students to select teachers.

Elective Programs. Some high schools offer elective
or phase-elective programs in academic areas, particularly in English and social studies. Students can choose
from a variety of minicourses, usually six, nine, or
eighteen weeks long. Other schools make minicourses
in all subjects available for a few weeks of the year,
often from the end of Christmas vacation to the end

of the first semester. Elementary schools offer minicourses too. Kennedy Elementary School in Lawrence, Kansas, offered a series of minicourses to improve pupils' self-images. Students in grades one through six could select from 80 topics, including motor mechanics, animal grooming, snake hunting, riflery, judo, billiards, and broadcasting.

Minischools or Programs. Some schools provide a program that is available by choice for all or part of the day; for example, a humanities course integrates English, social studies, and the arts for a half day in place of the usual separate classes. In an elementary school, open classrooms, Montessori classrooms, and conventional classrooms can be provided within one building. Parents select the one they believe is best for their child, but a child who does poorly in the program can be transferred to another program within the school.

Independent Study. Both elementary and secondary schools provide opportunities for students to explore in depth topics of their own choice. This can be arranged within a single class or classroom or through an interdisciplinary approach with several cooperating teachers. Sometimes independent study programs use learning contracts signed by student and teacher to define the area of study and the scope of the project.

Action Learning. Recently many public schools have begun to develop learning programs outside the school. These action or experiential learning programs go far beyond the typical work-study program for a few students or the occasional field trip for a class. Action learning experiences are intended for all students and would include internships within the community, social service programs, tutoring programs, student-conducted business enterprises, ecology and environmental programs, youth counseling centers, communications and arts programs, and other experiences that involve students in learning outside the school, usually for school credit.

These alternatives are available in some standard schools and some nonpublic schools, but undoubtedly more alternative learning experiences are available in the alternative public schools.

Alternatives to the Standard Public School

There is no standard definition for an alternative public school. One community's alternative school might be a standard school in another community. For example, an open school to which all the children in a neighborhood are assigned is not an alternative. An open school that is available by choice is an alternative school.

In other words, while no definition can encompass all alternative public schools, three criteria for determining whether a school is an alternative school are choice, difference, and representative enrollment.

Alternatives must involve choice. An alternative does not exist unless those it serves had a chance to reject it. Many fine innovative schools and programs are within public school systems, but unless the clientele that they serve have chosen that program rather than another one, they are not alternatives. In addition, the school must be different from the standard school in the community, and the enrollment usually should reflect the composition of the entire community, not a portion of it.

Characteristics of Alternative Public Schools

While each alternative public school has been developed in response to specific needs within its community, most schools have the following common characteristics. Any school lacking the first three characteristics would not meet the criteria for an alternative public school.

1. The school provides an option for students, parents, and teachers. Ideally the choice is open to all so that the school has a voluntary clientele. When

a school system provides enough alternative schools so that every family has a choice, the standard school becomes an alternative, too, as it then also benefits from a voluntary clientele.

2. The alternative school exists because of a commitment to be more responsive than the standard schools to some perceived educational need within its community. Therefore, the school is different from the standard schools in the community in an identifiable way—in approach to learning, in curriculum, or in resources or facilities.

3. The school's population reflects the racial and socioeconomic make-up of the entire community, unless the school is designed for a target group that is not representative of the community's total population, such as dropouts.

4. The school provides opportunities for students and teachers to participate in decision making on the school's program and on their individual roles within the school. The result is more choice and more responsibility for each individual.

5. The school usually has a comprehensive statement of goals and objectives. While alternative schools are concerned with developing basic skills and preparing students for college or careers or both, they are also concerned with improving self-concepts; developing individual talent, creativity, and uniqueness; understanding and encouraging cultural plurality and diversity; and preparing students for various roles in society—consumer, voter, critic, parent, and spouse.

6. The school is flexible and therefore responsive to planned evolution and change. Because alternatives are being developed in the age of accountability, they rely on feedback and formative evaluation in developing and modifying curricula and programs.

7. The school is usually smaller than the comprehensive secondary school. The median enrollment in alternative public schools is less than 200.

8. Because they are smaller, alternative schools tend

to have fewer rules and fewer bureaucratic constraints on students and teachers.

Pascal and Miller have suggested twelve characteristics:

1. *Voluntary.* An essential element in any viable alternative program is the opportunity, the option, of choosing to participate.

2. *Stress Involvement.* Students, parents, faculty, community, and administrators are involved in planning, operating, and evaluating the program in one way or another.

3. *Locally Developed.* Each program is "home grown," reflecting the needs, interests, resources, and facilities in the area or district.

4. *Rearrange Resources.* An optional alternative program uses its resources differently from the regular or conventional program. Most function at or near the same funding level as the regular program, once start-up costs are met.

5. *Well-Defined Goals.* Optional alternative programs go through a planning and development process that evokes clearly stated purposes and objectives.

6. *Representative Enrollment.* Rather than serving only a selected target group of students with special needs, increasingly optional alternative programs seek to attract diverse and representative enrollments.

7. *Maintain Relationships with the System.* Consistent with the belief that reform of the present monolithic school system is needed, alternatives work to build a close relationship with the "parent" school or school system, using its resources, exchanging ideas, communicating successes and failures, and trying to involve faculty, students, and parents from the "regular" program.

8. *Depart Significantly.* By definition, an alternative program is a significant departure from the existing program.

9. *Teach Basic Skills.* Optional learning programs

offer basic subjects, but in personal and responsive ways. Attention to skills development and subject matter often occurs within a supportive web of goal setting, building on successes and strengths, supportive peer groups, and multidisciplinary approaches.

10. *Develop Talents and Interests.* Optional programs help students develop a sense of identity and personal effectiveness.

11. *Personalize Student Learning.* Optional programs put people—their interests, needs, and how they learn—at the center of things. Students are the focus for organizing the educational program.

12. *Meet Requirements.* Since the option is the student's basic program, it makes arrangements to meet state and local district requirements for accreditation, attendance, or graduation common in the school district or area.

Purposes of Alternative Public Schools

John Fritz, a Canadian educator who visited alternative public schools in Canada and the United States, identified four purposes or functions of alternative schools. Published in his book, *My Encounter With Alternatives,* these four purposes help to clarify the role of alternative public schools:

1. They provide continuing educational opportunities for students who drop out of or prove disruptive in the regular high school. Typically, alternative schools represent a "last chance" for such students to continue and perhaps complete their high school program.

2. They serve students who, for a variety of reasons, find the regular high school inadequate to their needs and who are interested in exploring opportunities in alternative schools. Some school systems view this function as a "retreading," because these students will likely return to the regular high schools eventually.

3. They explore possibilities in developing new

school procedures or plans for subsequent wider application in the system. Alternative schools function in this respect as "experimental laboratories," and occasionally become pacesetters or lighthouse institutions within the existing school system.

4. They develop alternative programs in keeping with the diverse needs of student clients and parental conceptions of the type of schooling preferred for their children. This function reflects the growing demand for diversity and plurality in school forms available to a community, in contrast to the fairly uniform process of schooling prevailing, by and large, in contemporary systems.

Types of Alternative Schools

Optional alternative public schools vary widely in structure, size, instructional program, curricula, and resources. They range from the multimillion dollar educational park to the one-room storefront dropout center. Although more than a dozen types of alternative schools can be identified, some schools fit none of these types, and other schools are a combination of several. Much terminology on alternative schools is confusing, both to educators and to the public.

The term *magnet school,* used frequently referring to various alternative schools, has lost its original meaning. All alternative schools are magnet schools in the sense that they are designed to attract students to them. *Magnet school,* in the original sense, is a school with a specialized curriculum designed to attract students. *Learning center* is used when the emphasis is on special resources to attract students.

When a community has alternative schools so that every family has a choice of schools, then the standard school itself becomes an alternative. In southeast Minneapolis, every family may choose from four different elementary schools, one of which is the standard school. This further confuses any typology of alternative schools.

Obviously, all alternative schools share with the standard school the goal of providing learning experiences that are responsive to the needs of their clienteles. But each alternative school attempts to respond to its students in at least one dimension that is significantly different from the standard school. In providing brief descriptions of the types of alternative public schools, they are classified in three dimensions— emphasis on instruction, emphasis on curriculum, and emphasis on resources. While many alternative schools differ from the standard school on more than one of these dimensions, classifying them this way clarifies their central purpose.

Emphasis on Instruction

Open Schools. Open education provides individualized or small group learning activities organized around resource centers within the classroom or building. Learning is individualized and noncompetitive. Students progress at different rates. Open education frequently has interage grouping—several grades working together on the same learning activities. Only rarely, if ever, would a teacher use large group or whole class instruction. The open classroom requires a high degree of structure and a teacher who can orchestrate many different learning activities at once. The teacher's role includes organizing resources, diagnosing learning needs, providing appropriate learning activities for individual students, and recording and assessing individual progress. Many open schools operate throughout the country today, but the majority have replaced the standard school, and students are assigned to them. Only a minority are true alternatives available by choice.

Continuation Schools. These schools provide for students whose education has been, or might be, interrupted before high school graduation: dropouts and potential dropouts, pregnant students and teen-age parents. The continuation school is one of the oldest forms of alternative education.

Instruction in schools for dropouts and potential dropouts is usually designed to be significantly different from instruction in the schools that the students came from so that students won't repeat the failure and frustration that caused them to drop out in the first place. Instructional programs vary from school to school, but they may include individualized learning packages, behavior modification programs, mastery learning programs, continuous progress or nongraded programs, contract learning, individual tutoring in basic skills, and programmed instruction.

California requires secondary school districts to provide continuing education for persons in each community who have not completed high school. With a national figure of one million dropouts a year, continuation schools are clearly needed.

Store-front schools and street academies are located where they are readily accessible to the dropout and limited in size so that they will not appear similar to the large comprehensive high school. Harlem Prep, perhaps the best known of the street academies, started as a nonpublic school with foundation funds but has now become part of the public school system, salvaging dropouts and preparing them for college.

A part of a continuation school may be *reentry programs,* an office centrally located within the community where a counselor is available to talk with dropouts about returning to school and other alternatives. In Seattle, reentry programs and continuation schools attracted 3,000 dropouts into the public schools in their first year of operation. The Metropolitan Youth Education Center, with four locations in Denver and Jefferson County, has served 25,000 dropouts since it was started by Colorado's two largest school districts in 1964. Graduates from Metro have entered colleges all over the country.

A few school districts provide *pregnancy-maternity centers* for continuing the education of some of the more than 250,000 school-age girls who become pregnant each year. In these centers pregnant girls who choose to attend can continue their academic work in addition to courses in nutrition, child care, and family living. Because the most difficult time for the young mother is after the child is born, some centers provide day care for infants. The mother can return with the infant or leave it in the day-care center and return to her regular school. Pregnant students learn child care by helping with infants in the day-care center. Some centers provide courses in family living, consumer education, and child care for both parents.

Some alternative schools are designed for still other approaches to teaching and learning. The Pratt/Motley Schools in Minneapolis are based on *individualized continuous progress*. Students move at their own pace with individualized instruction and individualized help from the staff. Walbridge Academy in Grand Rapids is based on *behavior modification* theory. From the moment the students enter the school, they are placed on a point-reward system, which both students and teachers accept as a worthwhile learning environment. While *Montessori schools* are usually found in the nonpublic sector, a few public schools are based on Maria Montessori's principles. She believed that children should learn by doing and that a school should develop responsibility, self-discipline, and good work habits. Teaching in her own school in an Italian urban area, Montessori developed remarkable insight into how children learn. She found, for example, that five-year-olds could learn to write (encoding), but that learning to read (decoding) followed learning to write by several months. The Montessori Alternative in Cincinnati is a K-3 public alternative school.

Free Schools. Although free schools are also found more frequently in the nonpublic sector, a few free schools are within public school systems: the Southeast Free School in Minneapolis, Earthworks in Ann Arbor, and Murray Road Annex in Newtonville, Massachusetts. Free schools operate with few constraints on students or teachers, so that students are free to plan and implement their own learning experiences, thus developing self-discipline and responsibility. This is in the tradition of A. S. Neill's famed Summerhill School.

Emphasis on Curriculum

Magnet Schools. Originally the magnet school term was used to designate a school with a specialized curriculum to attract students. The first magnet schools tended to be elitist. Walnut Hills High School in Cincinnati started in 1918 for the academically talented, college-bound students, and still serves this purpose today. The Bronx High School of Science attracts top science students from all over New York City. Several communities have *schools for the performing arts,* which attract students who are talented in music and drama. Today many magnet schools are available by choice to interested students. A few communities have developed *schools for world studies* to further international understanding.

Environmental Schools. Because of increasing concern about the environment and environmental deterioration, some communities have started alternative schools with a curriculum built on environmental concerns. Mathematics, English, history, and science are integrated and related to specific environmental projects.

Multicultural Schools. These schools usually serve a clientele from various racial and ethnic backgrounds. The curriculum is based on cultural pluralism and emphasizes racial and ethnic awareness. Some *bilingual schools* offer a bicultural curriculum. Agora, a multicultural high school in Berkeley, with about one-third each black, Chicano, and white students, has a curriculum with traditional subjects and innovative cultural courses, including Harlem Renaissance, Chicano Studies, Modern and Afro Dance, American

Folklore, Women's Studies, Mexican Folk Dance, International Cooking, and Human Awareness.

Fundamental Schools. In a few communities parents have insisted that the school district provide a back-to-basics school with emphasis on the Three Rs. The John Marshall Fundamental School in Pasadena is probably the best known of these. Frequently other parents in the same community believe that the standard schools have never gotten away from the basics. In Jefferson County, Colorado, the school board has established two fundamental schools and two *open living schools* which combine features of the open school and the free school.

Emphasis on Resources and Facilities

Learning Centers. These schools concentrate in one location special resources that could not be made available in every school within a school district. Historically, the vocational or technical high school with its special programs and equipment was an early form of the learning center. Recently the learning center has expanded to include a variety of new programs. Houston High School for the Health Professions is located at the Texas Medical Center in Houston, where all the resources are available to help students learn about health careers. The Automotive Transportation Learning Center in St. Paul provides opportunities for junior high students to study automobiles, to take them apart, and to learn about driving and auto maintenance.

Schools Without Walls. The school without walls is designed to use the community as a resource for learning. A student at Chicago's Metro High School might take a course in Marine Biology at Shedd Aquarium, Television Production at the NBC Studio, Creative Writing at *Playboy,* and Animal and Human Behavior at the Lincoln Park Zoo. Every community has its unique learning resources. In small rural communities, some students interview senior citizens to

discover and record the oral history and the folk tales
of the community.

Educational Parks. The educational park is the only
type of alternative that may be larger than the standard
school. It may house a variety of programs from
kindergarten or preschool through programs for senior
citizens and other adults. The Skyline Center in Dallas,
a fourteen-acre building complex on an eighty-acre
campus, houses Skyline High School, the Career Development Center, and the Center for Community
Services. Skyline provides resources and programs that
would not be feasible in every school: an aircraft
hangar and airstrip, courses in Greek and Swahili,
a computer center, and an adult vocational program.

Alternatives in Administrative Structure

As might be expected, a variety of administrative
structures are used in the various alternative schools.
Some alternative schools operate as *minischools* or
schools within schools using a few classrooms, a wing
of a building, or a separate floor in a school building.
Others are *satellite schools* in a separate facility with
administrative ties to a standard school. They may
share administrators, health and transportation services, secretarial and clerical services, or transcripts
and diplomas with the standard school. Of course,
many alternative schools operate as totally separate
and autonomous units.

A recent development is the complex of alternative
schools or minischools, where a number of alternative
programs are housed within one large conventional
school building. Haaren High School in New York
City, Quincy II in Quincy, Illinois, and Cleveland
Heights High School in Cleveland Heights, Ohio, are
all large high schools housing a group of minischools.
The conventional program may or may not be one
alternative.

Sometimes several nearby school districts cooperate
in developing an alternative school. This is common

in the development of area vocational schools or career education centers, but Philadelphia, Denver, and Hartford have developed other types of alternative schools in cooperation with neighboring districts.

Shantí, a school without walls serving the greater Hartford region in Connecticut, is cooperatively supported by the Hartford Board of Education and school boards in seven surrounding districts. Shantí is a Hindi word meaning "the peace that surpasses all understanding." The school started in the fall of 1971 after two years of consideration and planning by educators, parents, and citizens in the Hartford area.

Space for alternative schools is seldom a problem. In communities with declining elementary enrollments the alternative school is sometimes housed in a former elementary school—Ann Arbor; Bloomington, Indiana; Minneapolis; and Racine, Wisconsin.

Alternatives Outside of Public Education

Alternatives are now developing in nonpublic schools as well as in tax-supported schools. Historically, more experimental schools have developed in the nonpublic sector, and many credit recent development of nonpublic alternative schools for stimulating public alternatives.

Traditionally some private and parochial schools have paralleled the standard public schools, especially in the tendency to be college-prep oriented. Some nonpublic schools have always been based on the learning theory of the founder of the movement, as Montessori, Summerhill, and Waldorf schools.

Nonpublic *free schools* have blossomed since the 1960s. Parents whose children attend these schools seem guided by Neill's Summerhill philosophy and a concern that the public schools were not meeting their children's needs. The typical free school is small, frequently with a total enrollment of fewer than 30, with one or two teachers. Sometimes parent volunteers aid teachers or teach themselves. Usually tuition is charged, and parents form a governing board. A thousand or more of these small, nonpublic free schools may be in existence today.

The *freedom school,* started in a few northern and southern communities, was designed to meet the needs of black students and to further racial pride and awareness. It also sought to increase black participation in politics and economics. The freedom school, usually available without tuition, was housed in a store front or other available community space. Interest in freedom schools was a product of the civil rights movement of the 1960s, and most of these schools died with the decline of that stage of the movement.

The *Christian* or *"white" academy* was likewise a product of the 1960s, appearing mostly in the South when court-ordered integration was being implemented. In the North some parochial school enrollments increased for the same reasons. While many of these academies are still in operation today, their numbers and enrollments are not growing.

Commune schools are not new, but the number of young parents in communes may have been increasing for the last ten years or more. The commune is usually a product of the counter-culture, and its school reflects the prevailing values of the commune. No source of figures for the enrollment in commune schools exists.

Just as there are a few public fundamental alternative schools, there are a few *nonpublic fundamental schools* today, but their number is not growing noticeably.

While nonpublic schools enroll fewer than 10 percent of the school-age population nationwide, in some communities as many as 30 to 50 percent of all students are enrolled in nonpublic private and parochial schools. The very existence of nonpublic schools negates the conclusion that everyone is satisfied with public schools.

Alternatives Beyond the Secondary School

The past two decades have brought a dramatic increase in enrollment in postsecondary education, with the largest growth in community colleges, junior colleges, and vocational-technical schools. With more young people in college, alternatives in colleges have increased, paralleling the programs of alternative elementary and secondary schools. Alternatives in higher education are designed for two purposes: to make the transition from high school to college less difficult and to provide an alternative to the traditional academic program.

High school-college credit programs give opportunities to high school students to take college courses for college credit before they finish high school. In the University Without Walls High School program at the University of Minnesota, high school sophomores, juniors, and seniors enroll as full-time university students and contract with their high schools to fulfill high school graduation requirements through college courses that will also carry full college credit. Thus students are working on the high school diploma and the college degree simultaneously. Most students enrolled in the first year of the program came from high schools that already offered alternative programs.

Some universities offer Upward Bound or similar programs to help disadvantaged students make the transition to college. The Thirteenth Year School in Boston, now called the Center for Alternative Education, is a private school designed to help students with weak academic records prepare for college entrance.

The *middle college* is another transitional program. Simon's Rock College in New York accepts students from the sophomore year in high school through the sophomore year in college with a program designed for 16- to 19-year-olds.

A consortium of 18 institutions of higher education created the Union for Experimenting Colleges and Universities to encourage innovation in higher education. One of the alternatives is the *University Without Walls* program which provides credit for off-campus learning experiences throughout the world. These opportunities may be available at one or more of the participating colleges or universities, in travel and service abroad, and in areas of special social problems. The programs have abandoned age grouping, fixed curricula, grades, and credits, and the classroom as the primary vehicle for learning. The University Without Walls emphasizes student self-direction in learning while maintaining close relationships among students, teachers, and resource people both in and out of the university community. Before completing a degree, each participant is expected to produce a major contribution—a research study, a work of art, a community service, a publishable book or major article, or some other noteworthy accomplishment.

One new experimental college, Governor's State University in suburban Chicago, is attempting to translate all courses into autotutorial learning packages to individualize learning so that professors can concentrate on individual counseling and tutoring.

Some universities are developing off-campus degree programs for both graduate and undergraduate students, while others encourage undergraduate students to take a year off to work, granting college credit for the year.

Alternatives to Schooling

In 1971 Ivan Illich recommended the deschooling of society by developing cooperative learning networks without certified teachers, school credit, or diplomas. While Illich's ideas have not gained general acceptance, some interesting attempts to provide informal learning opportunities have appeared.

As mentioned in chapter I, the Supreme Court gave

the Amish an alternative to compulsory schooling by ruling that Amish youth could learn informally within the Amish community instead of being compelled to attend public secondary schools.

A number of *learning networks* are developing around the country. One of the most successful of these is the Learning Exchange of Evanston, Illinois, that serves metropolitan Chicago. Since the Learning Exchange was established in May, 1971, with a $25 grant and a file box, participants have registered for more than 2,000 learning topics. The Learning Exchange has names and phone numbers of resource people with the abilities, skills, and interests to provide services. Interested persons of any age contact resource persons to learn about fees or required materials and to organize the learning experience. Anyone can be listed in the Exchange Resource file. Governor Dan Walker of Illinois said, "The Learning Exchange has proven itself to be an exciting alternative to formal classroom education. This unique educational program has given many people an opportunity to learn subjects not usually offered in the curriculum of most schools."

Free universities are another informal alternative. The free university usually operates on a college campus and offers noncredit courses free or for minimal fees. Courses cover a wide variety of subjects but tend to be practical rather than theoretical—consumer buying and investment, jewelry making, yoga, belly dancing, bread baking, bridge, natural foods, and so on.

Conclusion

In summary, a wide array of alternative schools and programs have been born since 1970. Enrollment in all these programs is probably less than 2 percent of all students. It is probably too early to predict the future of alternatives, but the early widespread interest suggests that alternatives, in some form and at one

level or another, will be around for a long time to
come.

Today several school districts operate multiple optional public schools, including Berkeley; Houston;
Minneapolis; Seattle; St. Paul; East Lansing, Michigan; Jefferson County, Colorado; and Quincy, Illinois.
Chapter III shows how one school district, Grand
Rapids, Michigan, is moving from a traditional school
system where students were assigned to schools to
an open system where every family has a choice of
schools.

The Development of Alternatives in One Community

1976: Grand Rapids' Alternative Schools

Grand Rapids, one of the first cities to offer optional programs, now provides alternative schools from preschool through postsecondary education for more than 25 percent of the city's 40,500 students. Many of the early Grand Rapids alternatives were developed to appeal to special students, but the emphasis has shifted to the idea of providing learning options for all.

The district has developed twenty alternatives during the past ten years, and now has at least one alternative, in addition to the standard school, available for each grade.

The twenty programs include six preschool and elementary alternatives enrolling 1,200 students, thirteen secondary offerings with 3,300 enrollees, and one K-12 program, in addition to an ambitious adult education program. Approximately 300 students come to the alternatives from surrounding public school districts and private schools. The Community Education Program attracts an additional 8,000 youth and adults to high school level programs annually.

The alternatives range from programs with fewer than fifty students to one with more than 2,300. They vary from open, flexible programs to highly structured fundamental schools. The alternatives, housed in both conventional and nonconventional facilities, consist of both alternative schools and part-time programs.

School Without Walls

A community-based high school, City School, was started in 1974 for seventy-five students. The school was expanded in 1975, with more than 40 percent of the classes located away from the school and taught by community members who are not certified teachers. Courses are held in banks, funeral homes, hospitals, courts, and in a wide variety of social agencies.

Continuation Schools

Grand Rapids now has three continuation schools— two dropout prevention programs and a maternity school.

Walbridge Academy is one of the oldest alternative public schools in the United States. In 1965 the public schools, working closely with county juvenile authorities, developed a four-month program to rehabilitate students expelled from school so that they could return to the regular classroom. But students who participated in this program were reluctant to return to the conventional public school and with their parents began pressuring for an expanded program. School officials were becoming aware that a short rehabilitation program for disruptive students was largely inadequate in dealing with dropout problems and that more comprehensive efforts were required. By 1970, a broad-based community Alternative Education Planning Committee was established, and the rehabilitation program was transformed and made available to students in grades 6 through 12 by choice. Students can graduate from the program. Today it attracts inner-city students who are predominantly lower socioeconomic and minority youth.

Walbridge Academy also developed a unique curriculum utilizing behavior modification, individualized instruction, and performance contracting. Students

earn points by successfully completing learning packages and trade these points for a variety of rewards:
trips to Chicago, weekend camping trips, bowling,
and time in the school's recreation center. This center
has pool and ping-pong tables and other recreational
opportunities available only through the point system.
Students can also accumulate points for a week-long
camping expedition on Isle Royale at the end of the
year.

Street Academy: Formerly a Model Cities program,
the Street Academy is modeled after the Walbridge
Academy, the only difference being that the Street
Academy also serves delinquent students.

Park School: Located in Booth Memorial Hospital,
Park School is an alternative available to pregnant
students through grade 12. While students in Michigan do not have to leave school while they are pregnant, those who wish to may attend Park School
during their pregnancy. The school is available not
only to Grand Rapids students, but also to students
in nineteen area school districts on a nontuition basis.
In addition to instructional services and counseling
opportunities related to pregnancy, most of the students' regular studies may be continued. Students learn
child care, health care, and nutrition and utilize hospital facilities as a learning laboratory. The school also
provides counseling and teachers for homebound students after the children are born. Plans are being made
to expand the program to include a day-care center
and a program for young parents that would offer
opportunity for young fathers as well as young
mothers.

Learning Centers

Learning centers have become the major emphasis
in alternative education in Grand Rapids. Some centers
are complete alternative schools where students can
obtain all educational requirements, while others are
off-site alternative programs where students are trans-

ported to participate for only a few hours each day. The Educational Park involves both concepts, so that students may participate in either one or two courses or a complete program.

Environmental Schools: In 1972, concern for students who were identified on fifth-grade achievement tests as being more than a year ahead of grade level led to the development of the sixth-grade Environmental Studies Program. Designed to stimulate and challenge highly motivated students from all socioeconomic and racial backgrounds, the program is housed in two of the most interesting facilities in the city. One is in the John Ball City Zoo and has, of course, come to be known as the Zoo School. Here students study animal behavior, do case studies of the animals, lead guided tours of the zoo, and utilize the surrounding park for nature study, environmental tests, and outdoor camping. The second program is located at the Blandford Nature Center, where a plot of land is assigned to students for year-long observation, experimentation, and exploration. Students study wildlife, plants, and trees and become familiar with wonders of the Michigan forest. Both environmental study schools are highly individualized and emphasize independent study and projects. They also have many field trips and culminate their year with a week-long campout.

After the first year, seventh-grade learning centers were established in math and science to provide continued enrichment for students who completed the Environmental Studies Program. A year later, as students moved up a grade, learning centers were added in the eighth grade.

Educational Park: One of the most complex alternative schools in the nation, the Educational Park was established in 1968 to offer courses that could not normally be justified in each neighborhood school because of the need for expensive equipment or specialized teachers or because of low enrollment. Ed

Park, as it is called, provided a mechanism for voluntary integration and also helped enrich the secondary curriculum. The area of Black Studies is an example. With the rise of black power, cultural awareness, and increasing community involvement in public education, demands for black history, Swahili, and a variety of cultural courses appeared. Because few certified teachers were qualified to teach them, it seemed impossible to offer courses in all public schools. The Educational Park provided an effective means of meeting these requests by allowing students interested in Black Studies courses to leave their schools for classes at Ed Park.

It is open to all Grand Rapids area students. Utilizing a complex of community facilities such as the art gallery, civic theater, and junior college, students experience a high degree of independence while traveling to one or more of eighty offerings in its expanded curriculum. Enrollment has doubled during the last four years, bringing the daily attendance to a comprehensive racial mix of about 2,300 students. The Ed Park also acts as an administrative umbrella for several other alternatives:

Advanced Independent Study: Students develop in-depth learning contracts with the interdisciplinary staff of the program and participate in thorough study of a particular issue. Often these studies have an experiential component that takes the student into community agencies.

Early College Enrollment: Twelfth-grade students who are not challenged by the public school curriculum may choose to attend classes at the junior college and earn both high school and college credit simultaneously.

Art Studies: Talented, highly motivated students may choose to do advanced studies in the arts using off-site community facilities and resources. Students may work in painting, commercial art, sculpture, pottery, and jewelry at the Grand Rapids Art Museum and study theater arts at the Civic Theater and film making at the Public School Media Center.

Math-Science Learning Center: High achieving seventh- and eighth-grade students may participate in enrichment learning for one afternoon each week at the Ed Park. These programs grew out of the sixth-grade Environmental Studies Program to offer students continuing enrichment.

Center for World Studies: The center is an off-site alternative for students interested in in-depth study of international issues. Here students may earn credit in social science, science, humanities, and the arts with emphasis on critical thinking and independent study. The center is also becoming a community focal point for dialogue on international problems and issues.

Performing Arts Center: This program was developed for fifth- and sixth-grade students who are especially interested in theatrical arts. The weekly afternoon experience is an enrichment activity designed to provide opportunities for the creative child to explore roles such as writer, producer, set designer, actor, and dancer. The program is housed in the Civic Theater and utilizes the professional theater staff as instructors.

Bilingual/Bicultural Alternatives

Grand Rapids has had a bilingual program in English and Spanish for several years, and plans are in effect to develop bilingual educational programs in other languages to reflect the ethnic composition of the entire community. One, the *Spanish Bilingual Program,* is designed to meet the needs of low-income Spanish-speaking children who have difficulty with the English language. The children's dominant language is used as the medium of instruction. In a second program for children who speak a language other than Spanish or English, a *multilingual/multicultural center* started at Palmer School in the fall of 1976. Children who speak Polish, Dutch, German, and Latvian receive classroom instruction in their dominant language.

Fundamental· Schools

Grand Rapids provides two fundamental schools that differ somewhat from those elsewhere. One is a former parochial school that became part of the public school system. The other developed from consolidating basic skills programs in several elementary schools.

Southeast Neighborhood Education Center: This alternative school is housed in what was formerly a small Catholic school. Because of their satisfaction with the conservative program, parents of this school worked to make it part of the public system after financial difficulties arose. After negotiation, the school, including teachers, students, and parents, was accepted into the public domain, where it continues to operate with strong family support. This program serves a small number of children primarily from the immediate neighborhood. A great amount of parent participation has shaped the instructional program. Rigorous attention is given to self-discipline, patriotism, good behavior, and values education. Through individualized instruction, students are helped to achieve in traditional study areas.

Sweet Street Academy: Stimulated by a number of small programs in a few elementary schools, Sweet Street was initiated to consolidate these programs into one. Designed for students who have difficulty in the traditional school setting, Sweet Street Academy offers a highly individualized instructional program with a strong emphasis on self-concept and basic skills development.

Preschool Alternatives

The Grand Rapids system provides two preschool programs for four-year-olds—prekindergarten and Head Start. Both programs strive to increase the child's effectiveness in dealing with the present environment and later responsibilities in school and life.

Prekindergarten: More than 400 children enroll each year in one of the three prekindergarten classroom settings—self contained, open space, or Montessori. Each of five self-contained units houses a teacher, an aide, and approximately eighteen students. The open space design houses 200 children, who move between learning centers and interest areas. The Montessori program is based on the child's developmental needs for freedom within limits and guarantees exposure to materials and experiences designed to develop the child's physical and psychological abilities.

Head Start: Since Head Start began in the summer of 1965, the Grand Rapids Public School system and the Kent Community Action Program (CAP) have cooperatively provided a comprehensive program for eligible children. CAP maintains responsibility for parent involvement and for volunteer and social services components, while the school district provides the educational and medical, dental, mental health, and nutritional services. About 160 children enroll in Head Start every year. The program focuses on a series of developmentally oriented activities emphasizing communication skills.

Adult Community Education

Programs and services for the community are offered in more than 150 centers throughout the community. Easy availability and increased need for adults to acquire additional training and skills have caused the number of participants to triple in two years. Grand Rapids has one of the largest adult education programs in the United States. Classes are offered in hospitals, homes for the elderly, and factories, in addition to traditional school locations. Program evaluations have indicated a high degree of satisfaction and success. Evaluations of the program in homes for the aged indicated that after elderly students enrolled in classes, the death rate was significantly reduced. Basic education, adult high school, and junior college educational opportunities are provided to employees of area industries through on-site programs. Since the fall of 1973, the number of industries served has grown from eighteen to thirty-eight and full-time equated students from 382 to 1,400. The program has been selected by Ohio State University as a model of cooperation between industry and education.

Reasons for Success in Alternative Education

By the early 1970s, the alternative schools already established had an impressive list of accomplishments. The Ed Park had demonstrated that it could provide educational programs to large numbers of students at a lower cost per pupil than conventional schools. Transportation and registration processes had been successful in moving students to and from alternative and neighborhood schools, and surveys indicated strong parent and student support for the Educational Park, Park School for pregnant students, and Walbridge Academy.

The transition of the Grand Rapids Public Schools from a uniform educational program to a complex system of alternatives represents one of the most extensive school reorganizations to occur in public education so far. Several key issues can be identified to help explain the success of Grand Rapids in this reorganization.

Careful Planning

Alternatives in Grand Rapids have been carefully planned. Most have grown from needs identified within the school system by local planning committees. Some recommendations and plans were made as long as four years before the alternatives were started. This long-range planning resulted in solid educational programs that were quickly institutionalized.

Cooperative Relationships

Grand Rapids has worked closely with juvenile authorities, courts, hospitals, local businesses, service agencies, private institutions, federal programs, and surrounding school districts to develop high quality programs. The first alternative school, created in 1965 for dropouts, was initiated with assistance from the county juvenile court. A number of surrounding school districts cooperated with Grand Rapids by sending interested students to alternative schools on a tuition basis. Grand Rapids provides for its students and for 1,675 parochial school students a wide variety of special programs, ranging from physical education to driver education to "drown proofing," an intensive swimming program.

Since 1972, Grand Rapids has worked closely with the Indiana University Alternative School Teacher Education Program. The local schools have employed more than sixty-five I.U. interns to help staff alternative schools, and graduate interns have worked on the district Task Force and participated in creating six new programs. I.U. interns composed the majority of the staff during the first year of the City School Without Walls. The following year, the school was staffed with regular teachers and a new group of interns.

Grand Rapids has also worked closely with other Michigan school districts to help them establish alternative schools. The school system has hosted regional and state conferences and has provided opportunities for public school educators to observe the Grand Rapids innovations.

Funding

Finding funds for new schools and new programs within schools, whether conventional or alternative, is always a problem. When extensive external funding is necessary to start a new school or program, it may not survive after external funds run out. While some of the alternatives in Grand Rapids started with funds from ESEA and local foundations, preliminary plans provided for decreasing external funds and increasing internal funds. Within three to five years each alternative was on the regular school budget. Robert Stark, director of alternative education, firmly believes in local funding for alternative schools and programs. He says, "The entire alternative public school movement will be futile unless school districts develop plans to provide permanent support from the local operating budget."

With more than 25 percent of the district's students in alternative schools and programs, and with twenty alternatives being developed, marked shifts in student populations occur each year. To adjust to these changes in school population, resources for each school, standard as well as alternative, are shifted so that money follows students to the program that they select.

Systematic Development

While some school districts have moved into alternatives by creating many new schools in a short period of time, Grand Rapids cautiously chose to develop only one or two alternatives at a time and, if successful, move on to create additional alternatives. This systematic growth took approximately ten years to develop the district's twenty alternatives. This step-at-a-time planning, coupled with comprehensive evaluation, has culminated in a solid core of well-accepted alternative schools.

Grand Rapids has also experienced a "ripple effect." Success of one alternative school has led to parental and student pressure for additional alternatives. The sixth-grade environmental studies program is an example. Following its success, alternatives were developed for the seventh and eighth grades.

Central Administration

In Grand Rapids, alternative schools are perceived as an integral part of public education. As such, alternatives have enjoyed strong support from school administrators. In 1971, a district level administrative office for alternative education was established, and administrative guidelines were developed for all alternative school programs. This office developed effective management techniques for alternative schools, means of registering and transporting students, a system for reassigning resources, and a policy for rigorous accountability. The final success of alternative schools may well depend on other districts developing similar administrative techniques.

Evaluation of Alternative Schools

Grand Rapids has developed a districtwide evaluation program for alternative education so that careful documentation of the effectiveness of programs can be maintained. While the district has not attempted comparative studies of alternative and conventional schools, it has carefully monitored the development of objectives for each school and then evaluated each on its effectiveness in reaching its goals. In fact, the District Office of Planning and Evaluation indicates that this evaluation has led alternative schools to prepare far better descriptions of their goals than do their conventional counterparts.

Several alternatives have also undergone external evaluations. But evaluation is not limited to alternative schools. For the past five years, the Office of Planning and Evaluation has evaluated conventional schools to identify areas of need that might lead to developing new alternatives.

A survey of the findings of more than twenty alternative school evaluations resulted in these strengths in alternative education:

1. *Facilities.* Alternative schools and programs utilize facilities existing both in schools and in the surrounding community. In this way, the alternative schools seem to use facilities more efficiently than

conventional schools. In a time of declining enrollment, a major justification for alternative programs
is their cost effectiveness.

2. *Selection Procedures.* While all alternatives
emphasize choice, inevitably they have developed
screening processes. In addition to choice, some programs receive referrals from courts and conventional
schools. Regardless of the process, all use final screening to determine if the alternative appears to be the
most appropriate learning environment for a given
student. This final screening usually includes inter-
views with students and parents and involves both
investigating expectations of students and parents and
describing the educational program offered.

3. *Student-Adult Ratio.* Almost all alternative
schools and programs have a smaller student-adult
ratio than conventional schools do. Alternative education ratios range between 1 to 8 and 1 to 15. This
is accomplished in alternative education by supple-
menting teachers with student teachers, university
interns, aides, parent and community volunteers, and
specialists in various skill areas. Robert Stark, director
of alternative education, believes that the low student-
adult ratio may be the most significant aspect of
alternative education.

4. *Pupil Achievement.* Alternative schools have led
to success in four areas: increased rates of attendance;
decreased rates of suspension; increased social maturity, adjustment, self-confidence, sense of responsibility, and independence; and achievement scores
equal to standard schools in reading and mathematics.
In the alternative schools that emphasize remedial
work in skills areas, the scores of students who were
making little gain in regular schools were consistently
raised.

5. *Student-Teacher Relationships.* The program
strength most frequently cited by students, parents,
and staff is the student-teacher relationship. This,
again, is perhaps because of the small student-teacher

ratio, but the attitude toward students is of major importance. It was found that in alternative education:

a. Teachers treat students as people and treat them with respect.

b. Teachers establish warm, friendly, and even affectionate relationships with students.

c. Teachers allow students freedom along with responsibilities.

d. Teachers create a casual, low-pressure atmosphere.

e. Teachers show a genuine interest in students.

6. *Relevance.* Another frequently cited strength of alternative education programs is relevance. Students and parents appear to believe that most alternatives offer an education that is realistically connected with the student's future. Students can see how school relates to the real world and are encouraged to develop career goals. On-site, hands-on experience is a frequently employed technique in successful alternative education projects. Teachers appear to be more flexible and open to suggestions and change than teachers in conventional schools and often maintain more contact and involvement with parents and community.

Problems in Alternative Education: Certain problems appear frequently in alternative education:

a. Enthusiastic supporters want programs to expand too rapidly; when a program appears successful, there are immediate pressures to enlarge and expand the program.

b. Screening and orientation of students is sometimes haphazard. Selecting students who can benefit most by a particular program should be given higher priority.

c. Many alternative education programs suffer image problems because of poor communication of program goals, weak public relations, and an unfortunate perception of alternatives as a dumping ground.

d. Staff must become well acquainted with new

processes before they are implemented. (For example, behavior modification techniques can be ineffective or harmful if misused or used by teachers without proper training.)

e. Conventional schools may feel slighted by the attention, privileges, money, and facilities granted to new alternative education programs, with resulting antagonism.

Conclusion

"When I talk about alternatives, I don't mean one small program in a store-front school," said John Dow, deputy superintendent of the Grand Rapids Public Schools. "Quality education demands that every child have learning options, and that demands diversifying all of public education. This means alternatives for all, and that's what schools must work toward."

Grand Rapids has clearly demonstrated that school districts can create effective alternative learning options and at the same time develop the financial, administrative, and organizational strategies necessary for their operation. In this, the city is far ahead of most other school districts in the nation. It has demonstrated that with careful planning and systematic evaluation experiential programs can be created to enhance the effectiveness of education. As the last half of this decade begins, it appears that Grand Rapids may become a pacesetter for developments in public education.

4

Blending Learning in School
and Community

*A simple rule of thumb ought to be: Whenever you can
do a thing better in school, or a place called school, that's
where you do it. If you can do it better 'out there,' you
do it out there.*

J. Lloyd Trump

The most dramatic change in public education
in recent years has been the attempt to move
learning out of the classroom and into the
surrounding community. In the past, public schools
operated on the assumption that all formal education
should take place in school. Such an assumption is
no longer tenable. Authentic learning takes place in
various settings with different sources. Distinctive
kinds of learning exist, and each may suggest or even
require a particular setting. Some kinds of learning
are appropriate for classrooms and schools, but scarce-
ly all. Some learning demands books, dictionaries,
libraries, and teachers; other requires travel, experience, and participation. As schools seek to match
students with appropriate places and environments
for particular kinds of learning, an increase in action
or experiential learning will continue.

Some schools now offer a vast array of learning
experiences in the community. Students are learning
in airports, courtrooms, funeral homes, jails, and hospitals. They are doing volunteer service work in homes
for the aged, building houses, buying and selling real

estate, or conducting an archeological dig. Others are learning survival skills through desert hikes, mountain climbing, and extended canoe trips. Classrooms are moved out of the school and located throughout the community. Courses are taught by bankers, carpenters, doctors, editors, lawyers, nurses, plumbers, or mechanics. Other schools bring the community into the school by using community volunteers, by staffing in-school classes with professionals from outside public education, and by developing cooperative programs with labor unions, business associations, and other private and professional groups. All of these efforts have tended to break down the artificial dichotomy between life and learning that has characterized schooling in the past.

For the past 200 years educators have worked to improve education by improving classroom instruction. During the 1960s these efforts reached a peak of activity that was regarded as a curricular revolution. Modern math was developed along with new curricula in science, foreign languages, social studies, and English. Simultaneously, teachers were retrained to use both the new materials and an inquiry-oriented approach to learning. But these developments were focused on classroom learning—on enhancing existing courses or replacing them with better ones and on improving instructional techniques. The underlying assumption that characterized most reform efforts of the past 200 years was that learning takes place with a teacher in a classroom inside a school.

What is important today is that increasing numbers of school districts are now concluding that some learning can and should take place out of the classroom and away from the school. The development of community-based learning experiences includes schools without walls, social internships, career education programs, and a wide variety of action learning programs outside the school. While experiential learning is only beginning to be explored, several factors help

explain the importance of and the need for blending
learning experiences in schools with activities in the
community. Most of these factors are clustered around
issues relating to school, society, and contemporary
youth.

Issues in the School

A dichotomy has always existed between what
happens in schools and what happens outside. Educational literature abounds with reports describing significant omissions from the curriculum, especially in
the social studies and language arts. In these areas
almost all controversial public issues confronting contemporary society and certain categories of literature
are often ignored. This peculiar aspect of schools did
not happen by chance. One explanation revolves
around the aftereffects of two early conceptions of
learning, and another focuses on the inability of public
education to develop effective change strategies.

Obsolete Learning Theories

Two of the earliest theories of learning are mental
discipline and classicism. Proponents of mental discipline believed the mind was a muscle and set out
to develop this mental muscle through rigorous exercise. The more difficult and obscure the learning
material, the more the mind was exercised. This led
to emphasizing the dead languages of Greek and Latin.
Classicists believed learning should focus on the great
ideas of antiquity that have survived through the ages.
Once again, the emphasis was on the far reaches of
history.

While aspects of these early educational theories
have been disproved and given way to more experi-
mentally sound theories of learning, they have left
their mark. School learning continues to focus on the
past, and too often teachers use drill and memorization
of abstract information as their main instructional
techniques. Most unfortunate, a startling credibility

gap between what students learn in school and what they learn outside of school continues.

Institutional Change Strategies

The weight of tradition, graduation requirements, college entrance requirements, state laws, teacher certification requirements, and textbook publishers have combined to solidify the school curriculum and its resistance to change. The result has been an ever-widening cultural lag between contemporary society and the school curriculum. Most educators agree that the school curriculum used today was developed for a society that has not existed for many years.

Issues in Society

The growing urge to get youth out of schools and into direct experiential learning situations is not based solely on the limitations and narrowness of school curricula and in-class learning, but is directly related to social transformations outside the school. Society is alive with technological changes that have ripped apart the social order and plunged everyone into a chaotic world that crackles with future shock. A survey of the effects of these social manifestations offers compelling arguments for blending the school and community in more intimate and effective ways.

The Society As an Information Source

James Coleman has argued that today's schools are obsolete because they are still trying to perform the information-giving function that they were initially developed for. Yet the information-poor society that spawned this particular function in schools has been transformed into an information-rich environment filled with multimedia sources that are far more relevant than the drab textbook and teacher sources typical of school classrooms.

Social Change

This is an age of unprecedented social change. While social change is certainly not new to western civilization, the change occurring during this century has characteristics that make it distinctly different from any previous era. This vertiginous change has rendered many of the most traditional values, institutions, vocations, and life-styles obsolete and dysfunctional. The effect on schools has been pronounced, for it has dramatized the liability of the school curriculum.

Proliferation of Knowledge

Ninety percent of the scientists who have ever lived are now alive and working in laboratories. The products of their energies have resulted in an explosive proliferation of knowledge. The entire body of knowledge appears to be doubling every three to five years. As new knowledge is developed, former theories and understandings are rendered outmoded and obsolete. Myths and superstitions are shattered, and ideas taken as universal truths have been severely questioned, if not destroyed. Schools once again have suffered from these effects.

Community Social Needs

The social needs of communities are becoming increasingly acute. Problems of community renewal, the environment, and social service have created social needs that far outstrip resources of state and local governments. This situation has been further complicated by rampant inflation and an increased competition for available resources.

Society can no longer permit schools to segregate the rich resource of youthful energy. The great curriculum question of the seventies is how to get students out of schools so that their energy, intelligence, and idealism can be used for social reconstruction.

Issues of Contemporary Youth

The nature of youth today offers further support for complementing in-school learning with a variety of community-based learning experiences.

The Dejuvenilization of Youth

School is unsuited today for assisting youth in obtaining some of the most important learning goals. It seems especially ineffective in helping in the social development that moves the child through adolescence and into adulthood.

Schools continue to deal with youth as unresponsible children, while in fact they have changed in the same dramatic fashion that Coleman argues the society has. Society seems to be "dejuvenilizing" youth. Outside the school, young people exercise considerable self-determination and are involved in life-shaping decisions; inside the school they are expected to obey. A number of recent conferences and national reports have focused on the biological and social changes affecting today's youth, and their conclusions are remarkably similar. All seem to agree that "the young aren't as young as they used to be."

A 1973 conference report, *The Greening of the High School,* summarized the biological transformation that youth is experiencing. Girls' menarche occurs two to five years earlier than in the past, and the voice change in boys is occurring just after 13 years of age compared with the average age of 18 in the eighteenth century. Venereal disease is replacing chicken pox as the most prevalent childhood disease. The rate of illegitimate births has more than doubled since 1940, and more than a fourth of all high school age girls are married. Yet, in some schools youth are not permitted to study even such topics as sex and social disease, and the authoritarian atmosphere of most schools squeezes out student efforts to assert their adulthood.

The Isolation of Youth

Today's schools have also tended to isolate youth from contact with adults. Especially during the past twenty years, as more and more youth have stayed longer and longer in school, teenagers have been increasingly separated from meaningful contact with adults other than parents and teachers. The fact that a student successfully completes high school will invariably be accompanied by a "decoupling" of the generations. It will also mean that youth will have delayed entry into the adult world, prolonged institutional controls over their lives, and lost the early transmission of adult cultural patterns. This situation has created a whole age group with minimum social controls subject to faddish whims and imprecise adult models. John Henry Martin, chairman of the U.S. Office of Education's National Panel on High Schools and Adolescent Education, believes that schools have been turned into "social aging vats" isolating adolescents and delaying their learning adult roles, work habits, and skills. Experiential learning outside the school offers an important means of eliminating the isolation of school-age youth.

Conflicts of Youth

Youth today are also different from preceding generations in more than biological terms. Because of the rapid rate of social change, Margaret Mead characterizes them as immigrants in time, like the first generation born in a new country and "faced with a future in which they cannot know what demands will be placed upon them." Constantly faced with problems without precedents, they have become perpetual adolescents in an era of unpredictable change. Thus, confined to life in an unfamiliar setting, they find few guides or models to direct them. This is especially true of life within schools.

Developing New Programs that Blend School and Community Learning

At best, schools have focused their educational activities in the cognitive area and have been fairly successful in this enterprise. They have transmitted a portion of civilization's cultural heritage, provided a working knowledge of the academic disciplines, and helped some students develop a desire for acquiring more skills and knowledge. In other areas schools have not functioned well. They have not provided extensive opportunities for students to manage their own affairs and to participate in intensive long-range study in a specific area. In addition, schools have become inappropriate settings for nearly all objectives involving responsibilities that affect others. The Panel on Youth of the President's Science Advisory Committee was concerned that schools monopolize too much of youth's time addressing a narrow range of objectives and thereby retard transition to adulthood. To correct this situation, schools have begun developing distinctive new programs that blend school and community learning experiences and that address a wide range of educational objectives, including social development.

The Cultural Walkabout

Writing in the May, 1974, issue of the *Phi Delta Kappan*, Maurice Gibbons proposed a unique new educational role for schools in assisting youth in their transition to adulthood. He based his conception on the Australian walkabout, a six-month-long endurance test during which the young aborigine must live alone in the wilderness and return to his tribe an adult or die in the attempt. "The walkabout," says Gibbons, "could be a very useful model to guide us in designing our own rites of passage. It provides a powerful focus during training, a challenging demonstration of necessary competence, and an enrichment of community life." What would such a walkabout be like for students

in American society? Gibbons gives some suggestions:
1) It should be experiential, and the experience should
be real rather than simulated. 2) It should be a
challenge that extends the capacities of the students
as fully as possible, forcing them to consider every
limitation they perceive in themselves as barriers to
be broken through. 3) It should be a challenge the
students choose for themselves. 4) It should be an
important learning experience in itself. Gibbons suggested that such an experience could be identified
and planned during the eighth to tenth grade and
become the primary educational challenge in the
youth's life. Gibbons organized the walkabout experience around several broad areas:

> *Adventure:* a challenge to the students' daring, en-
> durance, and skills in an unfamiliar environment.
> *Creativity:* a challenge to explore, cultivate, and
> express their imagination in an aesthetically pleasing
> form.
> *Service:* a challenge to identify a human need for
> assistance and provide it; to express caring without
> expectation of reward.
> *Practical Skills:* a challenge to explore a utilitarian
> activity, to learn the knowledge and skills necessary
> to work in that field, and to produce something
> of use.
> *Logical Inquiry:* a challenge to explore one's curios-
> ity, to formulate a question of personal importance,
> and to pursue an answer or solution, wherever
> appropriate, by investigation.

New Roles for Youth

The National Commission on Resources for Youth
is a New York-based organization that has surveyed
public schools throughout the United States to identify
programs that place youth in nonstudent roles. In a
small book titled *New Roles for Youth in the School
and Community,* the National Commission describes

a number of new roles for youth that would encourage
them to be responsible for their own welfare and the
welfare of others, orient them to productive and responsible tasks, and provide opportunities for learning
through action and experience rather than being taught
in a school classroom. The roles are designed to reduce
the isolation of youth from adults and from productive
tasks in society and to bring a greater degree of personal
responsibility for the development of youth. The
National Commission on Resources for Youth has
identified the following new roles for youth that are
being provided by special school programs.

1. *Youth as Curriculum Builders:* In the past,
regardless of what other privileges or opportunities
were granted to students, curriculum development
was left exclusively to teachers and outside experts.
A number of high schools have broken this tradition
and discovered that students work with diligence
and discipline, and they seem to enjoy the tasks
immensely. Schools have also discovered that the
young curriculum developers not only have produced high quality products, but also have gained
educationally from the process.

2. *Youth as Teachers:* The idea of students teaching students is as old as education and is used
throughout the world. Yet in this country the concept
has never been extensively used. Since 1960, interest
in youth teaching youth has increased, and a fair
amount of positive research supports this idea.

3. *Youth as Community Workers:* Schools have
begun to develop programs designed to involve
school-age youth in community service projects.
Such projects include assistance to mental hospitals,
homes for the aged, museums, day-care centers,
public transportation, and health and sanitation
facilities, to mention only a few. These programs
have had a positive effect on communities where
they have been created and give participating stu-

dents a sense of responsibility and accomplishment that schools have never provided.

4. *Youth as Entrepreneurs:* During recent years, some schools and other youth-serving institutions have been persuaded or even compelled to take advantage of the energy and enthusiasm that the entrepreneur role stimulates in many students. The resulting projects have included operating restaurants, rent-a-kid programs, house construction projects, urban renewal contracts, day-care centers, and even window washing.

5. *Youth as Community Problem Solvers:* Students can be utilized to identify pressing social problems, to conduct in-depth research on the problems, and to mobilize political support for possible action.

6. *Youth as Communicators:* Adolescents have developed newspapers, published books and magazines, made films, and created information centers and learning networks.

7. *Youth as Resources for Youth:* Young persons have also developed and operated crisis centers to assist drug users, runaways, and other troubled youth. They have established "crisis-line" switchboards operated twenty-four hours a day.

Career and Vocational Education

Career and vocational education offer almost unlimited opportunities for blending school and community learning and have the added incentive of being encouraged by federal funds. In a bold step to move vocational and career education out of the usual work-study half-day programs, the Office of Education has developed an Experimental Community-Based Career Education that is much more than a terminal program for students not college-bound. A far cry from on-the-job training, this program defines careers broadly to mean "one's progress through life" or "life paths"—not just a particular nine-to-five segment of

it. It enables students to complete the last two years
of high school by using extensive community experience, independent and group study, and maximum
out-of-school activities. Most important is that graduation requirements are based on "survival competencies" rather than course completion.

One Office of Education program, located in Tigard,
Oregon, allows students to leave school during their
last two years for a variety of community experiences.
Students complete a comprehensive battery of tests
to determine interests, abilities, and needs, then use
a computer-based survey of careers through which
they experience several career positions. Next, in-depth
experiences are chosen in a particular career area.
During this time each student completes ten projects
and thirteen competencies in three areas: basic skills,
career development, and life skills. During this two-
year period students do not attend classes but demonstrate their competencies in areas it is assumed most
Americans should master to function effectively in
their daily lives. Each competency is judged by a
selected community adult. Examples of the competencies follow:

Competency	Certifier
Transact Business on a Credit Basis . . .	Local Bank Official
Maintain a Checking Account in Good Order	Local Bank Official
Provide Adequate Insurance for Self, Family, and Possessions	Insurance Agent
File State and Federal Income Taxes	State and Federal Tax Employee
Budget Time and Money Effectively	Home Economist
Maintain the Best Physical Health and Make Appropriate Use of Leisure Time	Physical Therapist
Participate in the Electoral Process	City Recorder
Respond Appropriately to Fire, Police, and Physical Health Emergencies	Fire Prevention Officer, Police Officer
Understand the Basic Structure and Function of Local, State, and Federal Government	

. . . . . Local Government Representatives, Judge, Lobbyist
Explain One's Legal Rights and Responsibilities . . . Attorney
Make Appropriate Use of Public Agencies . . . . County Clerk
Make Application for Employment and Successfully
   Hold a Job . . . . Employer with whom Student is Working
Operate and Maintain an Automobile
   . . . . Driver Instructor, Police Officer, Mechanic

Another impressive career education program is at
Skyline Center in Dallas. In a school cooperatively
staffed by professional teachers, craftsmen, and skilled
professionals, students may survey as many as twelve
career opportunities during one year.

Another important program in operation since 1919
is Junior Achievement, in which students use consul-
tants from the community to assist them in organizing
a business, producing and marketing a product, and
generally participating in the entire range of experiences associated with running a company.

Other schools have utilized high school internship
programs that allow students to work directly in a
variety of professions.

Action Learning Programs

During the past few years, the National Association
of Secondary School Principals has exhibited a growing interest in out-of-school learning experiences. The
Association, along with the National Commission on
Resources for Youth, surveyed public schools and
identified action learning programs now operating.
Some action learning programs are:

Outdoor Learning Programs. Use of the outdoors
as a learning environment has experienced tremendous
growth in recent years. School districts across the
country are beginning to utilize the geographical assets
of their areas through hiking, backpacking, bicycling,
canoeing, caving, and camping. Some programs have
attempted to use the cultural neutrality of the outdoor
environment as an ideal place for confronting racial
antagonisms.

Following initiation of a wilderness program at Northwestern Junior High School in Battle Creek, Michigan, to alleviate racial and class conflicts among students, discipline referrals of a racial nature decreased 75 percent.

The Cambridge Pilot School in Massachusetts taught inner-city youth lacking in academic skills the techniques of outdoor education, then used these students as guides and teachers for more academically able students.

Probably the best known outdoor education program is Outward Bound with headquarters in Denver. Outward Bound has helped schools throughout the country to develop programs involving students and teachers in outdoor situations where they are faced with seemingly impossible tasks that call upon the maximum in personal reserves and individual perseverence.

Cross-Cultural Exchange Programs. Some schools have developed action learning programs to immerse school-age youth in cultures different from their own. Students at East High School in Denver have harvested beets with migrant workers, worked in welfare agencies, served food in soup lines, spent weekends on a Navajo reservation, lived with Mexican families, and collected garbage with city sanitation workers, all for high school social studies credit. In Lincoln-Sudbury Regional High School near Boston, students lived for five weeks with black inner-city families while working in social agencies, followed by five weeks in the remote rural settings of Connecticut and Nova Scotia where they worked on farms, in dairies, at maple syrup factories, and at organic food cooperatives.

Services Programs. One of the most practical and potentially valuable action learning experiences uses secondary school students as volunteers in community agencies and programs. Students volunteer their time and energy to work in hospitals, homes for the aged, drug centers, mental health clinics, and other social agencies. Some students have even organized their

own agencies and offer services within their communities. At Adams City High School in Colorado, students leave school to work as tutors and teachers for
second and third graders, providing elementary teachers with needed assistance. The Yorkville Youth Council in New York City uses adolescents as teachers and
tutors. Student volunteers in Marion, Indiana, have
become an important part of the staff at the local
V.A. Hospital.

A number of drug programs use high school students
as counselors, and some programs were planned,
developed, and operated completely by high school
age students.

One of the most dramatic examples of the potentiality
of youth volunteers was the Community Medical
Corps, organized in the New York Bronx. In the early
1970s, a group of medical students recruited 110 high
school students from 14 to 17 years of age to help
screen children in local tenements for traces of lead
poisoning. After a rigorous orientation session, the
students received white medical jackets and began
canvassing neighborhoods and conducting blood tests.
By the end of a summer, the students had seen more
than 3,000 children and had taken 2,000 blood samples.
More than 2 percent of the children tested had dan-
gerously high levels of lead poisoning. "High school
age youngsters had proved that they could be depended
upon to do difficult work," reported the National
Commission on Resources for Youth. "Many of them
had come into the program originally with an awe
of doctors and what they did. By the end of the summer,
the directors reported, 'We had kids telling the doctors
what to do. They had assisted with blood-taking
hundreds of times and knew the job as well or better
than any doctor.' The kids who worked here, all of
the 110 kids, know more about lead poisoning than
most doctors."

As a result of the program, many students are now
determined to become nurses, teachers, social workers,

and doctors. The program verifies the assumption that adolescents thrive on meaningful work.

Construction and Renewal Programs. Students have also entered into action learning projects designed not only to be financially rewarding, but also to beautify and renew their communities. In Denver, a group called Creative Urban Living has negotiated contracts totaling more than a quarter of a million dollars to build and refurbish houses, replace several blocks of city sidewalks, and construct several miniparks for the city. The students keep records on banking, payrolls, bills, loans, and insurance, and even publish a newsletter.

In Minnesota a group called Teen Corps organized 350 teenagers to provide volunteer labor for worthy projects in the state. The students built five summer camps for mentally retarded youth, a home for juvenile delinquents, a social center at a migrant worker camp, and an inner-city park. In Sacramento, California, volunteers age 6 to 80 visit welfare recipients' homes and assist in refurbishing and repairing houses. In Canton, Ohio, high school students have worked for twelve years in a Candlelight Youth Corps, renovating houses of the handicapped, the elderly, and the blind. Students also built a house and two duplexes and sold all three. Similar construction projects have been formed in Mollala, Oregon, in LaPuente, California, in Indianapolis, and in other school districts throughout the country.

Travel Programs. A few schools have organized traveling learning experiences to combine academic study with on-site visitation and experience. St. Paul Open School students have traveled to the Dakota Badlands and to the Gettysburg battlefield to combine geological and biological lessons with study of culture and history. In Lake Geneva, Wisconsin, a group called the American Essence Traveling School offers a program for high school seniors and graduates in which they spend nine months crossing the United States by rail, highway, footpath, inland waterways, and even wagon trails. The program is an in-depth immersion in America's heritage so that participants will gain a deeper commitment to the future based on a personal awareness of the past. Many schools, of course, have much less ambitious programs of weekend travel and summer experiences.

Political Programs

Armed with the right to vote at age 18, high school students have moved with an interesting display of force into the political arena. Students of East High School in Denver went to Greenwood, Mississippi, to assist in voter registration. The Connecticut Citizens Action Group, the first state affiliate of Ralph Nader's Center for the Study of Responsive Law, provided a model for youth participation in communities across the United States. Students in Connecticut conducted a state survey of food prices, developed an Earth Platform for election campaigns, and lobbied state legislators for a disposable bottle tax. All this has been done after school and on weekends without school credit. In other states students are being used as a pool of volunteer workers to gather information, conduct surveys, and utilize their information to influence voters, candidates, and legislators.

Another program that involves students in action learning in the political arena is the Washington, D.C., Street Law Program. Offered as a high school course for students in the D.C. area, the program is built around sixteen law students from Georgetown University who teach "street law" courses, which earn credit for both the high school students and the law students. Using discussion groups and special projects, the course culminates with students conducting a simulated trial with a federal judge leading the proceedings. The program has become a model for courses in other school districts.

Community-Based Schools

Earlier, several alternative public schools closely related to community life were described. A large number of alternative schools have been housed in noneducational facilities located throughout the community. Schools have been housed in former warehouses (St. Paul Open School), train stations (Shanti School in Hartford, Connecticut), hotels (Brown School in Louisville), and a wide variety of store fronts and office buildings. Aase Eriksen of the University of Pennsylvania has developed a model called Scattered Schools for utilizing refurbished residential housing scattered throughout the community.

Many schools without walls base curriculum in available community space and utilize noncertified teachers. Often courses are taught by bankers, lawyers, probation officers, social workers, or anyone with expertise in a specified area. The first school of this kind was the Philadelphia Parkway Program, but now schools without walls can be found in Chicago, St. Louis, Ann Arbor, Grand Rapids, Seattle, and other cities.

Organizing for Experiential Learning

Experiential learning poses difficult scheduling and organizational problems, for schools were not designed to provide community learning. Few schools have used Ed Meade's suggestion that schools act as "brokers for sending youngsters to and from the 'real world of experience.'" A number of ways of organizing experiential learning programs are:

1. *Course Supplements:* Often experiential learning has been developed as a supplement to regular classroom work or as a component of a particular course. Teachers often use experiences to illustrate particular concepts or as a way for students to learn particular skills. A history course may have a laboratory component in which students collect oral histories

of the great depression by interviewing older people in a community. Students in a science course may take water samples in area lakes or study traffic flow for a government class.

2. *Course Replacement or Equivalents:* Some experiential learning may be substituted for a course or be used as its equivalent for graduation requirements. A student can earn English credit as an intern at a television studio, a newspaper, or magazine. Science credit can be earned by participating in a university or private research project. Social studies credit can be earned through work in a courtroom or by doing volunteer work in a service agency.

3. *Semester Experiences:* A number of schools have created a "senior semester" or a semester-long "sabbatical leave" for students to participate in extensive out of school experiences. These include travel, rigorous outdoor learning programs, or cultural exchanges.

4. *Year-long Experiences:* Because many youth take off for a year or so before going to college, some schools have actively assisted students in planning a more productive year off. Some schools have organized the curriculum so that students complete all graduation requirements by the end of the eleventh grade, thus enabling them to participate in an extended independent study or a cultural walkabout experience. Many of these experiences are organized as postsecondary education programs and often involve travel and cross-cultural experiences. Theodore Sizer has called for a national conscription for all young men and women between the ages of 15 and 21 to spend twelve months in service to the community, asserting that the possible educational gains from community experiences are so important that they cannot be left to chance.

5. *Adult/Community Education:* Many major school districts offer community education programs that focus on adult education needs. Truly reflecting the "cradle to grave" concept of education, these public

schools have developed literally hundreds of courses available for community members. Originally pioneered in Flint, Michigan, by the Mott Foundation, community education has swept the country, offering courses wherever a need or interest appears. Courses can be found in hospitals, rest homes, factories, and community centers. Some programs even schedule classes for the home-bound.

6. *External School Experiences:* Perhaps the closest approach to Illich's deschooling idea is represented by the external degree programs under which high school diplomas can be earned without attending school. Five counties near Syracuse, New York, are now developing a program where students can earn a high school diploma without ever stepping inside a high school.

7. *Nonschool Learning Experiences:* Some of the more creative community learning experiences have been organized outside public education. Some communities have developed ad hoc learning-exchange networks. In San Francisco, community volunteers established The Switch Board, an informal system of putting people with learning needs in touch with resources in the area. Recently, a number of these community learning networks have been established with funding from the Federal Post Secondary Education Act. Some programs utilize local public libraries or other community agencies rather than public schools as the center for activities. While these programs are still in their infancy and usually focus on "supplementary learning," they do offer an important opportunity for evaluating this approach.

Blending School and Community: Some Reservations

While interest in blending school and community is increasing, it has been approached with caution by public school educators. The following caveats reflect their primary concerns:

1. Experiential learning outside the school poses extremely difficult scheduling problems for public schools that were not designed to provide for out of school experiences. The usual course schedule of daily, 50-minute classes poses almost impossible difficulties further complicated by logistical problems: how to develop flexible transportation systems to move students throughout the community and effectively monitor their work.

2. While research available on experiential learning is generally favorable, the question of legitimacy is still raised. Many still question whether these programs really belong in schools. Some believe other existing community agencies should be responsible for experiential learning or that new agencies should be created.

3. Many experiential learning programs are expensive. The National Commission on Resources for Youth recommends that all experiential programs be financed by student fund-raising projects.

4. The most difficult problem of all is the question of availability of opportunity. All existing community-based programs are small, and many are only pilot projects. What happens if all or even a major proportion of students begin to be involved? The organizational and administrative problems are overwhelming, even without the added problem of finding available learning opportunities outside the school.

5. Credit and state regulations can pose a serious restraint. A number of state departments have begun to develop guidelines for crediting experiential learning, but much work still needs to be done. Even more difficult is the question of accountability. These issues must be resolved before experiential programs can be organized, administered, and evaluated effectively.

Conclusion

The growing number of public schools that operate programs closely blending school and community learning is impressive. Because they are smaller and have fewer logistic problems, alternative schools offer better opportunities to organize action learning programs. In spite of administrative and organizational problems encountered by such programs, school districts have continued to develop closer relationships with community activities and experiential learning. These activities may represent the most important and productive area of educational reform and promise the most dramatic departure from the tradition of public education.

5

Pluralism in Education: Replacing the Melting Pot

The noblest aspect of the American liberal tradition is its respect for diversity. And this is not very likely to be fostered in a single setting, a unitary schoolhouse.
Theodore R. Sizer

The trend to diversify educational opportunities has provided a new dimension to the difficult issues arising from cultural pluralism in the United States. This is especially important because no other aspect of contemporary American society has proved as frustrating and frightening as the difficulties surrounding racial and cultural pluralism. The issue has literally exploded in recent years over the question of integration versus segregation, the debate about cultural assimilation or separation, and a spate of volatile issues varying from demands for ethnic studies in schools to conflict over the question of genetic inferiority of certain racial groups.

For twenty years these issues have been fought out in Supreme Court cases, local school board meetings, and even in classrooms. Through it all, the focus has sometimes been on education: demands for ethnic studies, bilingual education, integrated schools, and so on. While everyone acknowledges the problems, productive proposals for remedying the situations have failed. For this reason, the development of educational alternatives is especially important. This area holds promise for productive new approaches.

The need for pluralism is becoming ever more apparent in American education. Because a primary function of schooling is socialization, the appearance of increasing numbers of educational options suggests a dramatic shift in the purpose of education: Schools are beginning to reinforce differences rather than conformity and are strengthening diverse ethnic and cultural identities. Here is a contribution to the development of educational options that is almost overlooked.

Cultural Pluralism

The most obvious characteristic of contemporary American culture is that it is a pluralistic democracy, a tangle of competing and overlapping subgroups, all pushed together to clash over shared and disputed goals. A remarkable collection of the world's peoples are held together by the flimsy thread of tolerance, tradition, and geographic proximity. America is a cultural collage of black and white, young and old, elite and alienated, the very rich and the very poor, Democrats and Republicans, rednecks and radicals. Americans speak many languages and worship many gods. Each subculture has its own unique history and traditions, customs and tastes. Unfortunately, their values are often offensive to one another.

Given such remarkable differences, the question that has confronted educational institutions and quite literally torn communities apart is the role and purpose of public education. Should the schools function to assimilate these cultural differences and seek a degree of value consensus, or should the schools seek to legitimize diversity? For most of American history, the schools were the primary social agent for achieving cultural assimilation. As such, public education was perceived as the great cultural "melting pot" of society.

Schools as the Melting Pot

It was, of course, a beautiful dream. The schools were to take people of all races, all colors, all incomes, and all faiths and bring them together in a cultural harmony of equality and community. In the 1850s, public education became a cultural melting pot and worked to assimilate its diverse clients. Migration to the United States until the late nineteenth century was predominantly from England and northern Europe. By the time immigration from other parts of Europe and the world became substantial, the language and tradition of the white Protestant were clearly established. Thus, for economic and social survival and upward mobility, members of other ethnic groups were faced with the task of assimilating into a dominant culture. The task of accomplishing this assimilation was assumed by the public schools.

The schools often provided the first real contact between an immigrant family and the new society, and the white Anglo-Saxon Protestant (WASP) culture was clearly evident. Regardless of the widespread diversity of American culture, public schools developed around one basic educational curriculum. And whatever degree of diversity existed in school curricula had been eliminated by 1900 by uniform graduation requirements and state laws. Schools have always used the English language exclusively, and research during the last hundred years has clearly depicted the American school curriculum as amazingly uniform nationally. For more than a hundred years students have studied WASP history, read WASP literature, and been taught WASP values. Both the overt curriculum and the hidden curriculum exuded the values and norms of the dominant culture. Students learned to speak proper English, appreciate good literature, and behave properly, all judged by the inevitable standard of WASP culture. And, amazing as it seems, the melting pot really worked—at least for some.

It is estimated that the United States absorbed more than 40 million immigrants between 1880 and 1920. "The public schools did a magnificent job of molding and adjusting millions of immigrant children to their new role as citizens of the new country," Mark Krug

wrote in the 1973 Yearbook of the National Council
for the Social Studies. "Public schools were the basic
workshops of American democracy. It is in schools
that children of many racial, ethnic, and religious
origins learned, however painfully, to live together
and to take advantage of the precious gifts of American
freedom. Subsequently, the public schools made it
possible for thousands of Jewish, Polish, Italian, and
German children to attain positions of prominence
in all walks of life."

While many members of ethnic minorities managed
to disappear into the larger society, not all minorities
managed with equal success. Some remain culturally,
socially, and economically isolated even today. Among
these unmelted numbers are groups who have been
in the society from its beginnings: blacks, native
Americans, and Mexican-Americans. These unassimi-
lated groups share one basic characteristic: they are
physically different from the dominant cultural group.
As Jessie Jackson has said of these groups, "One half
of our population is still unmelted; it stuck to the
bottom of the pot."

The melting pot concept posed a number of difficult
dilemmas and contradictions. The core concept of the
Anglo-Saxon tradition in America is that every individual is able to rise to the level of his or her own
innate ability, to fulfill individual potential through
free movement upward. The schools were the major
means for achieving individual potential. Thus, people
were all to strive upward, and the best would always
win. This upward striving was to result in a melting
of the diverse cultures. Most important to this concept
was the belief that racial diversity was irrelevant to
upward mobility; all that was necessary was hard work
and motivation. Unfortunately, this aspect of the
American dream proved to be a humiliating myth for
most of the physically different minorities. In reality,
upward social mobility demanded far more than the
hard work and motivation myth of the melting pot

concept. It demanded that ethnic group members not only work hard; they were quite literally required to abandon their heritage and betray family loyalties. It demanded conformity to the biological and social norms of the Anglo-Saxon culture. "To succeed, to move into the dominant class, the individual (of ethnic origins) must abandon most of the cultural traits of his home," explains Mildred Dickeman, professor of anthropology. "Those behaviors, values, and attitudes which he abandons are those emotionally imbedded, acquired . . . in infancy and early childhood. To do so, he must disrupt his ties to his group of origin. What is demanded is a rejection of his affiliation with kind and community, of his ties to his group of birth." Thus, the melting pot concept was built on a subtle blend of shame and hope—shame in one's ethnic culture and hope for a better life.

To succeed in school and in the larger society, members of ethnic groups often changed their names, their language, and always their accents or dialects. They took on different styles of dress and developed new manners, a new family structure, and new values and attitudes. Even so, the dream of assimilation was still unattainable for certain groups. For them, a bitter realization that social assimilation was not enough set in. What was demanded was biological conformity, which for most was impossible.

The 1970 report of the NEA Task Force on Civil Rights stated that minority groups had had the choice of disappearing into the mainstream of American life or being "isolated and relegated to second class citizenship—or no citizenship at all." Most blacks, native Americans, and Mexican-Americans have concluded that they can never become white middle-class Americans.

One final paradox of the melting pot concept needs to be mentioned. As some ethnic group members embraced the Anglo-Saxon norms, changed their names, and severed their relationships with their ethnic heritage, they lost their group identity and their group power. The more assimilated a group became, the less political power it had in dealing with the dominant culture. Thus, even winning meant losing.

Problems of the Melting Pot Concept

In recent years the melting pot concept has begun to fade. A decade of protest and publicity has dramatized the plight of the nation's minorities. The growing awareness and acceptance of cultural diversity has begun to be reflected in the school curriculum. Increasingly, schools are offering elective courses in cultural studies, and new units have begun to appear in social studies and English classes. Textbooks, too, have developed multicultural illustrations and content.

Cultural Humiliation

When ethnic group youths were unable to assimilate, educators seldom questioned the institutional programs that had always worked so well for the middle class but assumed that something was wrong with the ethnic youths rather than the schools. In striving for cultural conformity, schools have often equated being different with being deprived, disadvantaged, or ignorant and have associated the minority with inferiority. Typical of a prevailing attitude that Indian homes and minds are empty and cultureless is the comment of a school administrator on a Sioux reservation, who said, "His home has no books, no magazines, radio, television, newspaper; it's empty! He comes to school and we have to teach him everything."

Inner-city youth are similarly viewed. "In discussions of education for the socially disadvantaged there is a good deal of sentimental talk about the 'valuable' or the 'positive' characteristics of the cultures from which these children come," Robert Havighurst reported in the *Journal of Negro Education.* "However, there is substantial doubt that the socially disadvantaged children in our big cities have any positive qualities or potential value in urban society in which they are systematically better than the children of families who participate fully in mass culture."

Such attitudes led to school programs and practices that humiliated ethnic youth. They taught students that nothing that they brought to school was worthwhile: not their history or their heritage, not their music, their language, or their folklore. Such children found themselves engulfed in the most traumatic social conflict of their young lives. They were taught that if they tried, they could make it; yet no matter how hard they tried, they learned that they could not succeed. They were encouraged to speak differently, act differently, and dress differently. For as long as they remained in school, they suffered bitter humiliation. Native American and Mexican-American students are still not allowed to speak their native language in many schools and are still punished in some if they do.

Institutional Racism: Selecting, Certifying, and Sorting

Institutional racism can be defined as those organizational structures, practices, and traditions that result in an inequitable distribution of success to all clients. Schools have long functioned as racist institutions, selecting certain students for upward mobility, and certifying that they have accepted approved norms of attitude and behavior. Thus, the schools have preserved social stratification by limiting upward mobility.

Typically, students from ethnic groups who find the institutional culture of schools alien to their way of life do poorly. Reading and math scores for these students are drastically lower than their dominant-culture counterparts, and this discrepancy widens as long as the student stays in school. At the third grade a three-year discrepancy appears between the minority student and his white counterpart; by the seventh grade it has typically grown to five years. This has led to "opportunity" classes, tracking, and the inevitable stigma of being culturally disadvantaged.

For these students, the years of humiliation usually end in dropping out of school. It is estimated that the dropout rate nationally is between 25 and 30 percent for all students. Nearly 80 percent of Mexican-Americans in Texas and California fail to complete high school. More than 60 percent of black Americans fail the Selective Service mental test, and the education of all Mexican-Americans averages only the eighth grade. A similar, if not more tragic, situation exists with native Americans. A 1969 report titled *Indian Education: A National Tragedy, A National Challenge* said:

> To a substantial extent, the quality and effectiveness of Indian education is a test of this Government's understanding and commitment. The few statistics we have are the most eloquent evidence of our own failure: Approximately 16,000 children are not in school at all; dropout rates are twice the national average; the level of formal education is half the national average; Indian children, more than any other group, believe themselves to be "below average" in intelligence; Indian children in the twelfth grade have the poorest self-concept of all minority groups tested; the average Indian income is $1,500—75 percent below the national average; his unemployment rate is 10 times the national average. . . .
>
> These facts are the cold statistics that illuminate a national tragedy and a national disgrace. They demonstrate that the "First American" had become the last American in the opportunity for employment, education, a decent income, and the chance for a fulfilling and rewarding life.

In every real sense, the public schools have not worked to help assimilate these ethnic youths into mainstream America.

Segregation

School districts have done more than simply sort, certify, and select. Some have worked actively to segregate the racially and culturally different in separate schools. Only in recent years have court cases exposed the elaborate and complex maneuvering school districts practiced to keep ethnic students segregated, using facilities, curriculum, and staff of significantly lower quality. School districts have gerrymandered school boundaries, juggled financial reports, tampered with pupil accounting, rerouted school buses and even planned their building programs around segregation strategies. Such *de jure* segregation activities have now been defined and exposed by the courts. But segregationist activities have been so successful and reflect so vividly the prejudices of the dominant culture that the challenge of correcting situations found to be illegal has so far defied most ideas and efforts. Often the solutions have been just as cruel and far more traumatic than the *de jure* segregation. Inevitably, the courts have ordered districts to integrate their schools, often with surrounding school districts, through compulsory busing. And just as inevitably, violence has tragically accompanied forced busing.

The Search for Solutions

Having a monocultural school to serve a pluralistic society has created a number of extremely difficult problems, yet few promising proposals have been put forward.

A survey of professional publications analyzing the educational implications of a pluralistic culture offers a striking insight. All the writers, especially the ethnic ones, write with a frank and passionate zeal when enumerating the evils of the melting pot conception of public education; yet when they propose solutions, most of their recommendations are simplistic. Some even suggest that the evils of institutional racism cannot be corrected. Others suggest politicizing ethnic youth, or developing community control of schools, or using ethnic studies and textbooks and employing teachers who are culturally diverse. Resistance to the solution of forced busing is increasing. Most recommended solutions simply tinker with the monocultural, single institution of public education rather than calling for overall reorganization. For example, they would have *Silas Marner* replaced with *The Invisible Man*, the chronological history of the United States replaced with Afro-American history, or perhaps include famous blacks in the typically white history. They would replace one course or textbook or teacher with another ethnic course, textbook, or teacher. Few have recommended diversifying curriculum and offering freedom of choice as a solution to ethnic problems. The approach that is earning acceptance and acclaim, namely, generating truly pluralistic educational institutions, offers an important new hope for solving problems arising from institutional racism.

While it is only a beginning, a trend toward developing and legitimizing pluralistic education opportunities is clear. It can be identified within public education through the development of alternative optional programs and schools, bilingual schools, community controlled schools, and ethnic studies. It is still too soon to forecast accurately the full impact of these developments, because most communities have not yet incorporated any of these concepts. Those who have experimented have typically done so with only a few small programs. Some pluralistic ideas are still politically unacceptable. The voucher plan, for example, while attracting increasing attention, has been tried in only one school district in the United States (Alum Rock, California) and there only on a limited scale.

Still, from a dozen major school districts a clear conception emerges of how diversified pluralistic education might bring a transformation. Because of American tradition, it is difficult to conceptualize an educational process and organization where learning is not limited to a single linear program organized with twelve grades. But ample evidence suggests that communities can develop an educational mosaic with wide varieties of experiences. Like a complex educational matrix, learning options can be organized around different subject areas, varied teaching and learning styles, and distinct cultural concerns.

The Emergence of Pluralistic Institutions

A number of communities now have educational programs that encourage and legitimize cultural differences. One of the first to do so was Berkeley, California. After a charge that institutional racism in the schools had served primarily the white constituency, plans were made in Berkeley in 1971 to transform the monocultural single high school district into a pluralistic institution with more than twenty alternative schools. Concluding that racism was evident in all institutions of society, it was thought that the most obvious and disastrous racism was found in public education. For the first time people and groups completely outside education became involved, and a philosophy of pluralism began to emerge. In their experimental schools education plan the Berkeley planners stated:

> The concept of pluralism is essential for consideration as the society grapples with the process of moving from an historically racist and exclusive society to a more open, inclusive one. The steps along the way have included enforced polarization or segregation, support for separateness in educational organization (as seen in the band-aid intervention programs of the early sixties) and subsequent moves toward integration, which in the past have meant assimilation or a melting into the dominant culture. No more. Today, one by one, all ethnic groups are polarizing and are asserting themselves, lashing out against the long-standing dominance of the Anglo culture in this society. The desire to adapt to living in an overwhelmingly white environment is lessening and the interest in working at this is also diminishing.

Pluralism speaks to cultural diversity, viewing difference rather than sameness as a value. Pluralism demands that choices, options, and alternatives exist. It highlights the need for new approaches to education—not only new types of schools with new missions, but also new patterns of going to school and new ways of administering schools.

Despite all of its elaborate professional language, the institution of education mirrors society's view of itself. Just as white society finds it must respond to the pressures of minority groups, so education must look at the significance of racial identity as a thrust at racism. The most pervasive protest and the most difficult to communicate in terms of education is the revolution in racial behavior. The racial identity thrust of racial behavior, more than anything else, tests the American commitment to education as the only institution through which all children can share the wide range of experience that is both the richness and the poverty of American life.

To date it has been the common school to which the American dream has been hooked, and therein lies much of the problem with which the institution of education is struggling. The common school as we know it has not provided for pluralism in the populations of school communities. It has a built-in failure factor for a large percentage of its constituency, and this factor is necessary for its existence. Indeed the all-purpose school no longer exists, if it ever did at all. It hasn't delivered equality of opportunity, guaranteed an open society, or served as an equalizer. The school with a uniform standard for accreditation and human dignity is outmoded.

Since 1971, Berkeley has developed more than twenty alternative schools, providing a classic example of a pluralistic model for public education. Alternative schools are not just a few small programs for a few special students. In Berkeley, optional learning opportunities exist across the entire educational spectrum. The school district has taken the blame for achievement disparity between white and nonwhite students rather than taking the traditional route of blaming the culturally different students for this achievement gap. Also, the alternatives have heightened appreciation of differences and respect for the life-styles of different races.

Multicultural Schools

A number of public and private schools have been founded during the past few years with racial and cultural understanding as their primary goal. While still addressing the comprehensive goals of elementary and secondary education, these schools have developed their curriculum with an urgent concern for cultural awareness and understanding. Faculties and student bodies are multicultural. This usually means establishing quotas: some schools may be half-white and half-black; others will divide their openings into thirds and recruit white, black, and Chicano students. Schools with more diverse communities have other quotas to include—native Americans or Orientals. Agora and Franklin are two multicultural schools in Berkeley.

Agora. When Agora got under way in 1971, students were concerned because their staff and students were almost wholly of one race—white. They decided to adopt a multicultural identity and actively recruit nonwhite students and staff. The first step was a pilot project in which disenchanted students were recruited and near-miracles began to happen. A summer pilot program successfully turned nonlearners into learners.

This experience was the beginning of Agora's evolution into a center for ethnic awareness and cultural learning with an equal number from each race and a required course where all students rotated from one racial study to another.

Through the years, the ethnic awareness component has remained strong. About one-third of the students are white, one-third black, and one-third Chicano—but the emerging force is what was intended in the beginning—decision making by the students.

Classes at Agora include Harlem Renaissance, Geometry, Language —Tool or Weapon, Chicano Studies,

Algebra, Communication Skills, Basic Design, Black
Seminar, Soccer, Modern and Afro Dance, Math
Games, Art Workshop, Black Drama, American Folklore, Creative Writing, Women's Studies, Chess, Mexican Folk Dance, Music Performance, Spanish, International Cooking, Human Awareness, and Tennis.

Franklin Multicultural. Franklin grew from community demands for recognition of the special needs
of nonwhites. Asians, who reside in a larger number
in the Franklin-Jefferson area than elsewhere in
Berkeley, had long asked for a program that dispelled
stereotypes and brought Asian culture into the curriculum and consciousness of both staff and students.
Likewise, Chicanos had long complained that mono-
linguistic handling of learning left out their Spanish-
speaking children.

Out of these concerns the Franklin alternative school
was devised. After the first school year (1971-72), the
bilingual component of the alternative was deleted,
to be conducted at Franklin by the Bay Area Bilingual
Education League. This left the Asian cluster of four
classrooms and a seven-class component working on
individualized handling of each child's special needs
and a curriculum that emphasized cultures through
their respective contributions and history.

The two schools' components share common features, including: small groups for reading instruction;
personalized approach to children and their learning
needs; use of reading tutors; individualized counseling; openness to parents; frequent use of multicultural
materials; many cultural field trips; use of team teaching and of classroom instructional aides; stress on
life-related activities such as producing newspapers
and magazines; building projects; conducting classes
in local banks, stores, libraries, courts; and creative
activities such as writing radio programs, movies, and
dramatic performances.

Voluntary Integration Models

Recent studies by James Coleman have suggested that forced integration has been largely ineffective and that schools integrated by compulsory busing quickly become resegregated by population shifts. If this conclusion is correct, it creates a difficult vacuum, for integration by forced busing has been the primary means of the courts for eliminating segregated schools.

During the past few years, as court-ordered busing has unleashed reservoirs of bitterness and violence, a few school districts began exploring other methods of racial and class integration. One of the most promising ideas is voluntary integration by choice.

St. Paul Learning Centers. In the early 1970s, the St. Paul Public Schools created several elementary and secondary learning centers, seeking to ease segregation in the district. Fermin Alexander, director of the Learning Centers Program, said, "The emphasis of the Learning Centers integration model was on providing unique educational experiences which had not been available before. The emphasis was not on mixing bodies according to some arbitrary formula. The emphasis was on quality education available to all students in every school." Assuming that all parents wanted quality education for their children, the school district set out to create learning centers of such high quality that students and their parents would be anxious to volunteer for this program even though the students in the centers would be racially mixed.

Their organization was unique. Students still attended their local neighborhood school, but if they chose to, they could leave the local school for a half-day for short minicourses in the Learning Centers. At the end of the first year of operation, 97 percent of the elementary school children in the district participated voluntarily in the Learning Centers program, accomplishing almost total racial and class integration with few of the problems that have confronted other school districts. St. Paul had developed a formula for mass integration: all students still attend their own neighborhood school and were bused to an integrated program voluntarily.

While attending a Learning Center, the students are in a completely integrated situation. Each session has minority group children, low socioeconomic background children, middle-class children, and children from affluent homes. The most important feature of the program is that these students are enrolled in the centers because they want the unique learning experiences that are provided. The program is completely voluntary—no one is forced to attend.

Brown School; Louisville, Kentucky. In 1971, an alternative public school was organized in Louisville, and housed initially in a downtown hotel. The Brown School was composed of grades 3 to 12 and attracted students from throughout the school district. Most important, the school was designed to be half-black and half-white on the basis of established quotas. Any child in the district could choose to attend the Brown School as long as there was a vacancy in the appropriate racial quota. Thus, the Brown School was a multicultural school integrated by free choice.

The Brown School has become a model for school districts throughout the country in teaching effectiveness, curriculum, and innovative programs. The school has developed a comprehensive program for dealing with cultural awareness and racial conflicts between students.

During the 1974-75 school year, the federal courts found the area to be practicing *de jure* segregation and ordered the Jefferson County Schools and the Louisville Public Schools to integrate; compulsory busing was to be the means to bring about integrated education. Federal officials were perplexed about a school already integrated without compulsion. Initially the decision was simply to close the Brown School.

Finally, as a tribute to this creative program, the Brown School continued to operate the program of voluntary integration while the two districts were integrating by compulsory busing.

Private Free Schools

A classic example of the conflict between public schools and black communities is found in Boston. Jonathan Kozol described this situation in his popular books, *Death at an Early Age* and *Free Schools*. Kozol was fired from the Boston Public Schools for using the writings of Langston Hughes, the black poet, in his literature classes. Although the black students "turned on" to learning for the first time with black literature, he discovered that the material he was using was not on the acceptable list and he was ordered not to use it in his classes.

After he refused to comply with the school order and was dismissed, Kozol joined with the black community to create a private Free School in Boston. Since its creation, the Free School has come to be regarded as one of the finer examples of a private free school operating outside public education. It is deeply committed to cultural awareness and understanding and to teaching black students the basic skills they need to survive in a technological age. The school also works to politicize black youth and confront them with the realities of the white-dominated culture and racist institutions. In spite of the difficulties of economic survival of schools outside public education, the Boston Free School had demonstrated that important contributions to the development of pluralistic educational opportunities can be made by private schools.

Unfortunately, free schools outside public education have often continued racist educational tendencies. Kozol writes with a bitter rage in *Free Schools* about the middle- and upper-class students "off in the Vermont woods" shuttling their hand looms, weaving baskets, and making Iroquois canoes. He summarizes his point with cutting directness: "In my belief, an isolated upper-class Free School for the children of the white and rich within a land like the United States is a great deal too much like a sand box for the children of the SS Guards at Auschwitz." From Kozol's point of view, what inner-city youth need is not so much freedom, but hard work, drill, dedication, and political awareness. With the growing interest in voucher education, community-controlled private schools could well become an even more important part of the pluralistic educational opportunities available in communities.

The Politics of Pluralism

While increasing evidence shows a trend toward pluralistic institutions, ample evidence also indicates this trend is not without opposition, especially where racial minorities are concerned. Numerous times blacks have encountered difficulties in developing community control of schools and Indians have waged battles with the U.S. Bureau of Indian Affairs. The difficulties confronted by Mexican-Americans offer a vivid example of the opposition that minority groups have encountered when they have attempted to diversify public school programs.

Like the blacks before them, Mexican-Americans have made a unified effort in the struggle for social justice. They have already waged a national boycott against California grape producers; they have fought for and won departments of Chicano Studies in at least a hundred colleges and universities; they have gained an Office of Spanish-Speaking Affairs in the Department of Health, Education, and Welfare; and they have lobbied successfully for a bilingual education act. Perhaps more important, in countless squalid barrios scattered throughout the American southwest, Mexican-Americans are experiencing a dawning awareness of their plight, and with deep conviction and determination they have joined the battle in classrooms, school boards, and local elections.

Carrying the double affliction of a dark skin and a foreign tongue, the Chicano faces mammoth educational obstacles in American schools and universities. Unlike the black community, which has its own colleges and a small but solid elite of academicians, the Chicano culture lacks an intelligentsia of its own. There are no Chicano colleges and few Chicano Ph.D.'s. As late as 1965, very few Mexican-Americans had the Ph.D., and none were in fields of Chicano history, culture, or philosophy. Lacking Chicano scholars in these areas, their history has been largely unwritten, their literature remains uncompiled, and their philosophy has not been fully developed. Until five years ago, no Chicano Studies departments existed in the United States and in the whole country fewer than a half-dozen Chicanos were school superintendents. Before federal aid programs, few Chicano students ever made it to college. Although more than a million Chicanos live in the Los Angeles area alone, almost no Chicano students were in California state colleges before the advent of federally funded programs.

In public schools, Chicanos have fared no better. The 1969 Governor's report in Texas indicated that nearly 80 percent of Mexican-American children who started school in first grade failed to graduate from high school. In California, the Chicano dropout rate is more than eight out of ten. Nationally, the Chicano has an average education of only eighth grade, with 70 percent failing to graduate from high school.

In California, culturally biased tests used to track students have resulted in a large percentage of Chicano students being categorized as retarded. While many Chicano students relegated to special classes were not retarded when they entered those classes, by the time they dropped out of school, they were, according to standard achievement tests.

Chicanos have not only been forced to study in

classes conducted solely in English, but often have been punished for speaking their native Spanish. One can still see signs by phones in public schools saying "No Spanish calls to home," thus creating a difficult dilemma for the children whose parents know no English. Ill-prepared Anglo teachers, unfamiliar with the nuances of the Spanish pronunciation, not only have embarrassed students by their inability to pronounce Spanish names, but have forced Chicano students to respond to Anglo nicknames.

During the late 1960s and early 1970s, Mexican-Americans began to organize and exert political pressure on local public schools to diversify their curriculum and offer bicultural and bilingual education. One of the first areas where this occurred was the dusty, border towns of southern Texas. Towns with names such as Crystal City, Uvalde, and Cotulla erupted in open warfare during the early 1970s.

Crystal City, Texas, is an example. Until 1970, the town's only claims to fame were that it 1) was halfway to the Mexican border from San Antonio, Texas, 2) was recognized as the Spinach Capital of the world and has a statue of Popeye to prove it, and 3) once won the *Laugh-In* Show's weekly Fickle-Finger-of-Fate Award. Perhaps more important to the local residents is that 85 percent of the Crystal City population is Chicano.

Located in the Rio Grande Valley thirty miles from the Mexican border, Crystal City is the winter home of a major migrant work force. Owning no land, and staying in Crystal City only for the winter months, the Chicano has traditionally lacked residency requirements for voting. It was not until the late 1960s that a federal court declared that a nine-month residency would suffice for voting rights. To the ruling Anglo minority, this court order was an ominous warning, for it opened the possibility that their city might be controlled by transients who were only periodic visitors. It was this court ruling that set the stage for a major confrontation.

The public schools in Crystal City in 1970 were similar to most American schools for Chicano students. Almost all of the teachers were Anglo, and all classes were taught in English. Speaking Spanish was discouraged in the schools, no courses were designed for the Chicano majority, and no library books focused on the Chicano. Even the history courses had only passing mention of the heritage and culture of the Chicano. Nonetheless, the situations that finally catalyzed the Chicano youth were much more trivial concerns.

In mid-December, 1969, Crystal City Chicano students took the lead in mobilizing their numbers for political activism. Disgusted with school regulations designed to enhance the few Anglos in the schools, Chicano students led a walk-out, followed by a school boycott so effective that the entire school district was forced to close down. The rules that had antagonized the students were relatively minor compared to the total tragedies of their lives, but to the students they became the focus of their frustrations and growing anger. Of the high school's six cheerleaders, three positions were reserved for Anglos. Also, the homecoming queen could only be chosen from students whose parents had graduated from the local school; since few Chicanos ever graduated, the homecoming queen had traditionally been an Anglo. Viewing these rules as the final humiliation, the Chicano students walked out of school.

Discovering that three seats of the seven-member school board would be up for reelection in March, and because one Chicano already held a position, the community saw a chance to gain control of the policy-making apparatus of the schools. Sparked by this opportunity, the students began a comprehensive voter registration and voter education drive. They enlisted three local Chicano candidates, one of whom had been denied a teaching job in the school though he held a master's degree.

The Anglo minority, which had ruled for so long,

was surprised and frightened by the possibility that they might face a reversal of roles. The Anglo schools were closed, their teachers were out of work, and the threat of a Chicano-dominated school board was imminent. One local Anglo teacher said in shocked amazement, "Why—they're trying to take over!" Many Anglo teachers suddenly feared they would lose their jobs if the Chicanos won the election, and community leaders began forecasting social and economic doom if "those stupid people" gained control. Reaction was swift and sure.

On election day, an Anglo rancher was requested to move away from the polling area after he aimed a rifle at a Chicano candidate. Other ranchers, by driving their pick-up trucks almost bumper to bumper around the polling area, intimidated Chicano voters. Most of the pick-ups had gun racks with rifles over their rear windows. Finally, the Chicanos called upon the Texas Rangers as an uneasy ally to force the Anglos to cease heckling and frightening potential voters. Other Anglo ranchers sat across from the polling area with voter registration lists checking off the names of each Chicano who entered to vote. Throughout the election day, the wife of one candidate received telephone threats against herself and her children.

That night, as the election returns began to come in, it was apparent that the Chicano "children's crusade" was proving successful. Next morning, even though the Anglo judge refused to swear them in, the Crystal City School Board was composed of four Chicanos and three Anglos. For the oppressed majority, it was an important moment, both for Crystal City and the Chicano movement. In the five years since 1970, bilingual and bicultural teachers and curriculum have become a way of life in Crystal City. The educational program has been diversified to reflect more adequately the pluralistic composition of the community, and both Anglos and Chicanos have a more realistic, enriched learning experience. The previous uniform school program has given way to a more complex set of learning opportunities.

This educational revolution that began in Crystal City has spread across the southwest to Cotulla, Uvalde, and San Antonio. Similar educational reforms are under way throughout the west and southwest where public schools are giving up their models of assimilation and beginning to develop pluralistic programs emphasizing and encouraging cultural diversity. Particularly vital, these schools are developing the most important option of all—the opportunity to learn in one's own language and in an educational setting that reinforces one's own cultural background.

Conclusion

Crystal City dramatizes the turbulence of transitions that attempt to eliminate institutional racism from school districts. Such transitions are never easy. They are too often accompanied by conflict and bitterness. But school districts are being changed. They are slowly yielding to community control and participation: ethnic studies, bilingual programs, voluntary and compulsory racial integration, and a growing variety of multicultural concerns. All this, of course, is only a beginning, but it is a significant start.

The development of pluralistic school districts and the creation of alternative school programs appears to have played an important role in this beginning. The alternative movement has helped to legitimize and popularize pluralistic educational programs and provide a useful strategy for reforming school districts. Evidence suggests that the creation of a small multicultural school, a magnet school, or even a bilingual program provides a manageable and acceptable first step toward educational pluralism. As these small programs are carefully evaluated and their effectiveness demonstrated, they hold promise of becoming models for more widespread educational diversity. In Berkeley, St. Paul, Louisville, Boston, and Crystal City pioneer efforts are under way that could well dispel the myth of the melting pot.

6

The Right to Learn

S hould schools respond to the learning needs of children, or should children conform to the expectations of schools at the expense of learning? This question makes some principals and teachers uncomfortable and defensive, but it shouldn't. The truth is that the standard school is not effectively meeting the needs of some children and youth, and something can be done about this.

Historically, the function of the American school was to provide one type of learning experience—book learning, both as necessary to literacy and citizenship and as preparation for further schooling. It was always recognized that many students failed to benefit from the academic program of the schools. Society expected these students to leave school early and to find responsible jobs. Thus, a second function of the school has always been to sort out those who would not benefit from further academic learning, retaining and preparing an academic elite for higher education. But in a recent and dramatic turnabout, society today expects the schools to provide universal elementary and secondary education for all students, including those the schools were designed to eliminate. This is a real challenge.

Children learn in different ways and at different times, and a single child may learn in varied ways at different stages of development. While most educators and the public would accept these two assertions, their implication is disturbing. For many years schools have been attempting the impossible—to teach every child in the same way at the same time. What has been done in schools is inconsistent with the beliefs about learning. The reason is obvious. The traditional pattern of organization in the schools with all eight-year-olds assigned to one classroom was established many years before there was a psychology of learning.

If psychologists agreed on a single theory of learning, it might be possible to restructure schools to provide learning experiences that were congruent with this theory, but they don't. Several conflicting theories of learning, each of which influences instruction in different directions and suggests a particular alternative school, exist today: the behaviorism of B. F. Skinner, the cognitive development theory of Bruner and Piaget, and the humanistic psychology of Maslow, Rogers, and Combs, to mention three that seem to be conspicuously influential.

Much of what is known today about the human brain has been learned in the past few decades. It is doubtful that any existing theories of learning will suffice as knowledge of the brain's function and development increases. The present educational system may fail to develop the creative potential of the individual at the very time when it is recognized as society's most valuable resource.

Chapter 1 stated that the majority of children and youth are deprived of equal educational opportunity when they are assigned without choice to a standard public school. Equality of educational opportunity would require varied learning environments to meet the needs of diffferent students. Our present knowledge is inadequate to create an array of learning environments to meet the needs of all children and youth. The development of optional alternative public schools is one step toward providing schools that will be responsive to the needs of more students.

Before providing equal educational opportunities for all students, educators will have to find out more about the learning needs of students and the relationships between learning styles and learning environments. They will also have to dispel current myths about schooling and learning.

Learning Styles and Learning Environments

The academically talented were previously defined by James B. Conant as the top 15 percent in scholastic aptitude. Whether they are called the academically talented, the cognitively competent, the high achievers, or just the bright students is incidental. This is the group that does well in the conventional school curriculum. Many from this group will be college graduates.

What are the remaining 85 percent called? When teachers answer this question, they frequently use disparaging terms to describe this large group, which makes up the bulk of their students. Schools, particularly secondary schools, have focused on a curriculum for the academically talented student so long that they have not even identified the majority of the students, much less analyzed their learning styles. The result is unequal opportunity for the majority of students because they are not academically talented.

Most comprehensive high schools provide a general course of studies and a vocational program for students who are not college bound. But the majority of the course work required for the students in either of these programs is still academic.

This does not mean that only the academically talented are profiting from school. Indeed, many who have academic talent are not doing well in conventional schools, and some with great academic talent are among the million dropouts annually. It is the top 15 percent who are academically talented and academically motivated who profit most from the conventional school curriculum. But many other students who may lack academic talent but who have academic motivation also benefit. These include the students who are talented in a particular area—art, music, athletics, science—and who want higher education to further develop this talent. They include also many students of average academic talent who are highly motivated to go to college by family expectations or by interest in a vocation that requires postsecondary education.

But many elementary and secondary students are not benefiting from schooling now either because the academic program is unsuited to their learning styles or because they lack motivation for academic achievement. It is these students who need alternatives in education.

"It is possible that some models of teaching will have great effectiveness with some learners and very little with others," Bruce Joyce and Marcia Weil said in *Models of Teaching.* "Possibly any science of behavior that ultimately emerges will require us to learn about the differentiation among human beings as well as the regularities to which we are all subject."

The concept of matching instruction or the learning environment to the learning style of the student is very new in educational research. It may be many years before educators can diagnose an individual student's learning style and prescribe an appropriate learning environment, but promising research investigating the learning styles of students and their relationship to alternative and conventional schools is already under way.

The Conceptual Level Matching Model

During the more than ten years that David E. Hunt of the Ontario Institute for Studies in Education has been studying interaction of the person and the environment, he developed the conceptual level matching model for matching the conceptual levels of students with varying environmental structures. In 1975 he reported the relationship between students' cognitive orientation and the amount of structure in the environment, using two alternative public schools in the same community in a "twinning program" so that students and their families could choose according to their needs or learning styles.

Hunt specified four "accessibility characteristics" of students to coordinate with educational environments: cognitive orientation, motivational orientation, value orientation, and sensory orientation. His work is the first to deal realistically with the complexity of learner-environment interaction. This model will provide a valuable guide for analyzing the match between learners and various alternative learning environments.

Success in Alternative Schools

Robert Fizzell, director of the Action Learning Center in Niles Township, Illinois, reported in 1975 the characteristics of students who were succeeding in conventional and alternative high schools as a basis for matching learners with schools. He explored three areas: personal characteristics, academic characteristics, and external influences. Academic characteristics include innate characteristics, academic self-concept, learning style preferences, time structure preferences, and interests. By comparing profiles of successful and unsuccessful students in a school, critical differences between these groups were discovered and the implications for matching analyzed.

He found fifty variables related to success in school and made a startling generalization: Often characteristics associated with success in one school are associated with failure in another. If Fizzell is right, here is strong proof that equality of educational opportunity within one school is an impossibility.

On the basis of personality profiles, Fizzell generalized that the student who was average or mid-range on most personality variables would progress well in the standard school. The student who deviated on personality variables and had a "distinctive" personality would do better in an alternative school.

He also suggested ways certain alternative schools were matching the learning needs of students with certain measurable characteristics. For example, he suggested that open secondary schools "serve students who are academically motivated but frustrated by traditional structures."

Fizzell also identified the "loners," students who were not peer-oriented but who sought involvement in the adult world. These students did well in an action learning program that involved them in independent projects or work in the community. He also identified students who had done poorly in both the regular and the alternative schools. This justified his conclusion that "one alternative is not enough."

Fizzell has also described other types of students and groups of students that he found in observing alternative schools. His descriptions parallel those of Cusick, who in 1973 described student groups within the conventional high school. More research on subgroups of students within standard and alternative schools is needed to guide the creation of effective alternative learning environments.

In 1972 Sherman, Zuckerman, and Sostek explored the background and behavior of the anti-achiever and reported, "The most serious form of underachievement—the neurotic refusal to achieve—appears to have become more prevalent." At their Center for Alternative Education in Boston, a postsecondary program has been developed to meet the needs of the anti-achiever.

Reeves did a study in 1975 of disaffiliated students or dropouts in Grand Rapids. This study shows that 90 percent of the disaffiliated students want to return to school if the learning environment can be modified to meet their needs.

At present little is known about the relationship between creativity and either regular or alternative learning environments. Some believe the environment of the standard school stifles creativity. Samples made a strong case in a 1967 article that creativity was a severe handicap for the student in the conventional curriculum.

The relationship between hyperactive students and alternative learning environments needs immediate attention. Estimates of the number of elementary school children on drugs prescribed to control hyperactivity in the classroom vary from one million to six million. Schrag and Divoky reported in 1975 that this type of behavior control was affecting "primarily white, middle-class children." In one instance two parents, unwilling to submit their child to the drugs, requested that she be assigned to an alternative elementary program. In the alternative program, an environmental school with much outdoor activity and projects instead of academic work, the girl showed no signs of hyperactivity. Instead, she was quiet and cooperative and displayed a high degree of artistic talent that she had not previously displayed in the conventional classroom. While this single case does not allow a generalization, it does suggest the need for exploring alternative learning environments for students who are hyperactive in conventional class-rooms.

The Learning Needs of All Students

The relationship between the development of educational alternatives and the currently unmet learning needs of all students should also be given a high priority in the immediate future. The traditional function of schools was narrowly confined to one area—academic or cognitive development. Research on the human brain in the past thirty years has drastically altered the scientific view of the brain and its functions. Education and educational psychology still operate today under older doctrines that this research makes obsolete.

Roger W. Sperry, in a 1975 article summarizing

recent brain research, offers three conclusions:

1. [E]ach individual brain is truly unique. The
   degree and kind of individuality each of us carries
   around in his brain . . . would probably make
   those differences seen in facial features or in
   fingerprint patterns look relatively simple and
   crude by comparison.
2. [O]ur educational system and modern society
   generally (with its very heavy emphasis on communication and on early training in the Three
   Rs) discriminates against one half of the brain.
   . . . In our present school system, the attention
   given to the minor hemisphere of the brain is
   minimal compared with the training lavished on
   the left, or major, hemisphere.
3. One of the more important things to come out
   of our brain research in recent years . . . is a
   greatly changed idea of the conscious mind and
   its relation to brain mechanism. The new inter-
   pretation, or reformulation, involves a direct
   break with long-established materialistic and behavioristic thinking. . . . This swing in psychology and neuroscience away from hardcore materi-
   alism and reductionism toward a new, more
   acceptable brand of mentalism tends now to
   restore to the scientific image of human nature
   some of the dignity, freedom, and other humanistic attributes of which it had been deprived by
   the behavioristic approach.

Sperry's third point suggests a move away from
behavioral psychology, the psychology that still domi-
nates schools and the mainstream of educational psychology today.

The work of Jean Piaget, the Swiss psychologist
who has been investigating the cognitive development
of children for many years, has been the object of
much recent interest in education in this country.
Based on his work with Piaget, Hans Furth suggested

in 1970 that schools needed to develop cognitive rather than reading skills in the early years. Furth says he fears that the ways early reading is currently taught can be harmful to the cognitive development of the child.

The issue here is not whether Furth is right about the possible harmful effects of the present approach, but whether schools that concentrate on such a narrow range of mental development can continue to be supported at the expense of other areas. Many parents are concerned about the moral, aesthetic, and affective development of their children. These areas now get only minor attention, if any, in conventional schools.

"Although children are whole people—full of fantasies, imagination, artistic capacities, physical grace, social inclinations, cooperation, initiative, industry, love, and joy—the overt, and above all, the covert structure of our system of preschooling and schooling largely ignores these other human potentials to concentrate on cultivating a narrow form of intellect," says Kenneth Kenniston, chairman of the Carnegie Council on Children. "Our inordinate preoccupation with intellectual development and our presumption that it can be handily measured have not only shortchanged the general population of children in our schools but have also tended to hamper such efforts as we have made to give special help to those children needing it most."

But if all students need more effective programs, what role do alternatives play? In the past decade it appeared that it is difficult to change the schools to fit all students, since many students and their families are satisfied with conventional programs and resist changes. Nevertheless, alternatives can become laboratories for pioneering more effective programs. Because the alternatives are available by choice, only those families who want or expect changes will choose them. If and when the alternatives develop more effective programs that would benefit more students,

it will be much easier to move such programs into
the other schools. In fact, when parents of children
in conventional schools know that alternative schools
have more effective programs, they will insist on these
programs for their children, too.

Myths About Learning

"The principal came over to our house and told us that
we shouldn't let Junior (Willie) play baseball because
education was going to be more important for him in the
future than baseball," Willie Mays' sister said in a TV
interview.

To develop more effective learning alternatives, common myths about schooling and learning will have
to be recognized and rejected, including the following:

1. "Learning equals schooling and learning doesn't
occur outside of schools." A high school teacher
suggested to his principal that some students should
have the opportunity to plan and build a house for
credit. This had already been done in several other
communities. The principal responded, "If you give
them a choice between building and learning, they
will all choose building." This illustrates the tendency
of many today, including educators, to equate learning
with schooling or with academic classroom work. This
is a serious barrier. A much broader and more accurate
definition of learning will need to be developed for
the schools' clientele.

2. "Today's work force demands a large number
of academically trained people." Havighurst reported
in 1975, "The Department of Labor states that only
about 20 percent of the positions in the working force
require as much as high school graduation. Thus the
high school and the community college have perforce
become custodial institutions for a substantial proportion of their students."

3. "Those who stay in school will get better jobs
than those who drop out." In a feature article on

nonformal education, Thomas LaBelle and Robert Verhine state, "Investigations in the United States have determined that graduates of vocational programs are no more likely to be employed than are high school dropouts." At least one study indicates that dropouts are more likely to be employed that high school graduates who did not attend college.

4. "Conventional schools have considerable diversity—both in their instructional programs and in their effectiveness." Goodlad and Klein say of their study of elementary schools in 1970: "Our study reveals sharply that almost all of the schools we observed pursued a course of bland uniformity regardless of pupil population and school setting."

5. "The majority of high school graduates enter college." Forty percent of the males and 46 percent of the females in the class of 1975 planned to enter college. Another 5 percent of the males and 4 percent of the females planned to attend vocational schools. More than one million students drop out before high school graduation. This, added to the figures above, would indicate that approximately one-third of the age group plans to enter college today. Of course, not all who plan to, do so. Approximately one-fourth of the age group enter college the first fall after high school graduation.

6. "The schools are effectively meeting the needs of white, middle-class students." William Rohwer reported that 33 percent of white students from middle-class families are not attaining success in school.

An Agenda for Today

E. J. Duffy, principal of Glenbrook North High School in Northbrook, Illinois, suggested in 1974 today's most crucial educational problems:

1. Too many students are not motivated to learn.
2. Too many students lack the basic learning tools necessary for becoming lifelong learners.

3. Each student possesses a unique learning style, yet is required to adapt to whatever style the school imposes.
4. Most students lack a personal relationship with the teacher as a human being.
5. Traditional staffing arrangements impede efficiency in most individualized educational programs.
6. Learning strengths and weaknesses in the abilities of students are not identified or properly utilized when they are diagnosed.

The community should consider creating alternatives to respond to these crucial learning problems. As alternatives develop within a community, important issues about learning will require further exploration and analysis: Do alternatives respond more effectively to the learning needs of students? Which alternatives are for which students? How is the student's learning style diagnosed? Does a student have only one learning style, or are there different styles for different subjects? Does learning style change with time or with stages of development? How are learning styles matched with teaching styles? What are the relationships between school structure, teaching style, and learning style? What are the relationships among intellectual aptitude, learning styles, and motivational differences?

We must seek answers to these questions and many, many more.

7

Choice and Power

The Importance of Choice

Only in the past ten years have educators begun to realize the critical importance of affective growth. It has become increasingly clear that what a student thinks of the learning environment may be as important, if not more so, than what is cognitively gained from a given learning experience. The implication is that the attention paid to how people feel about their learning experience is just as important as that paid to cognitive growth and development in all content areas. Business and industry have recognized this condition for years. The higher the level of positive feeling, the better the performance. If people have a voice in how, where, what, and when they are teaching and learning, their attitudes will be more positive. At present, students and teachers in many, but not all, alternative schools have more choices about their educational experiences. This choice both aids the learning process psychologically and eases the crucial matching of teaching and learning styles.

A second reason that choice in education is important is that the corresponding responsibility or accountability for a given choice is shifted from the institution to the teacher or student or both. Because teachers and students have selected and agreed on objectives, one can no longer blame the other or the system for imposing an unwanted or undesirable structure.

Through this commitment, teacher and student may assume increased responsibility for their own activities. Additionally, people who choose to participate have a greater chance of success in an activity. What is devastating for either a teacher or student is to be led into thinking that a given experience is best suited to their needs when they actually know they are being manipulated.

Third, a new relationship between teacher, student, and parents forms a partnership in teaching and learning. Voluntary because all parties were involved in choosing, this partnership can develop mutual trust and respect, creating an effect of sharing and caring. A cooperative attitude and relationship may permeate the teaching/learning process.

Finally, the concept of choice is commensurate not only with democratic expectations but also with the real world that students are preparing to enter. Rather than preparing for it, students experience the real world within their schools.

Obviously, problems within the school setting are looked at differently because their resolution involves all parties. Greater loyalty is a characteristic surfacing in many optional alternative public schools. Self-examination and constant critique rather than criticism become tools and techniques that both students and teachers learn to respect and utilize.

Something is psychologically significant about the size of a school population. Studies indicate that the smaller the school unit, the more humane it tends to become. This does not mean that tutorial programs or one-to-one relationships are the best circumstances for teaching and learning. However, a school of 750 students is likely to have a more humane environment or feeling than a school of 3,000. The larger the school, the more bureaucratic it becomes, the more controls are needed, and the greater the structure, increasing the number of constraints. In short, humaneness comes closer to being reality in schools of choice than in schools where no choice is available for either students or teachers.

Some evidence shows that a higher proportion of students in optional alternative public schools continue longer with formal education than students in traditional schools. Frequently, this act of choice improves self-concept. Teachers and students in optional alternative public schools are beginning to realize the relationship between choice and learning. For example, Parkway in Philadelphia and Metro in Chicago, two alternative schools where students have many choices, send a higher proportion of their graduates to college than the other urban high schools in Philadelphia and Chicago.

Interestingly, the psychological aspect of choice has contributed to lower rates of absenteeism, fewer discipline problems, decreased truancy, and less vandalism, according to reports from several alternative public schools.

Too Much Choice?

Some critics argue that too many choices already exist and that a standardized, if not basic, educational system should be restored. As long as choices are available, it is acceptable, even desirable, to have some schools designed by choice for those who wish to have the basics emphasized. That choice clearly ought to be available in communities where such a need is articulated.

More practically, having too much choice can expose people to a variety of choices they know little about. Poor or incorrect decisions are generally made in one of two ways: first, people have inaccurate information or have misinterpreted information about an area of choice, and second, they have too little information upon which to make a judgment. Still another concern is that expanded choices cause people to pick randomly rather than carefully select an educational program.

Other dangers are inherent in making choices a

viable basis for creating an educational system. Consider these potential situations: Students who make choices that enable them to remain at a level of productivity below known capabilities; teachers who make choices based on personal bias and prejudice; parents who make choices for their youngsters based on "Joan did well in the open school, so Connie will, too," and so on. Nonetheless, collectively involving parents, teachers, and students in choice may minimize irrational decisions.

Finally, when can youngsters appropriately participate in the choice process? In some minds a six-year-old is incapable of making educational decisions. Some parents and teachers are comfortable with the concept of structured freedom, in which younger students have a few choices about their education, and as they mature, they are given more say about their learning environment.

Those who have a vested interest in whatever choice is made include the student, the educator, and the parent. At some point the parents' influence on decisions of their youngsters may become tenuous. When the student and parent have opposing viewpoints, the student's wishes generally will prevail psychologically, if in no other way. At this point, which well may be in the junior high school years, the student's power in making the ultimate choice about how he or she chooses to learn, if choosing to learn at all, becomes paramount.

The Community: A New Responsibility

Separating the school as an entity from the community is neither defensible nor desirable from an educational viewpoint. The community, including parents, is the single most overlooked educational resource. The diversity within the community can and must be reflected in the schools. Legal and financial responsibilities for public education lie directly with the community through an elected or appointed board of education. The business community employs the products of the school and therefore must have input. Above all, the graduates of the public schools become the citizenry of the community without whose blessings, at least financial, public education will suffer. Once students leave school, they become the governing bodies—the voters and board members. Without a global view of the schools' relation to the community, public education will continue to suffer through bond issue defeats, operating levy defeats, and serious declines in morale.

So many complex issues appear within communities, including political cleavages, vested interest groups, social cliques, and a host of other concerns, that school officials seldom experience long enough tenure on the job to begin to deal with the community as a power base, educational resource, or copartner in building better lives, futures, and values. Only when educators become community leaders and the school becomes a community interest will educational agencies and their communities gain the values of a partnership. The optional alternative public schools are based largely upon grassroots efforts. Many have been founded by parents and community groups. In these schools, a truly exciting relationship has taken form, but not without new struggles and problems, however. Many people, educators and the public alike, agree that they are ready to exchange the present set of problems for a new set, primarily because the new problems are educationally relevant and are affecting the lives of people, both in and out of school.

Just as there are politics of change, so are there social and psychological aspects of making school-community relations work to the welfare of each. In at least two ways alternative school personnel are engendering better school-community relations: First, school personnel are going out into the communities rather than always insisting that people come to the school. This is psychologically important, because

going out of the school lessens the defensiveness of
the educator and enhances the receptivity of the public.
Second, the public is being invited to become an active
participant in the actual learning settings both in and
out of school. This means they can become a part
of the school as aides, resource persons, or observers.
For the first time in American educational history,
parents and the public are beginning to believe they
are part of the school system. The resulting partnership
is reported to have considerable effect on school-community relations, on teacher morale, on student interest
and performance, and on broadening the educational
resources only lightly tapped previously throughout
the community.

The political overtone here is one of simple public
involvement. Participation can mean better definition
of problems, more open discussions, and keener application of accountability measures. Just as with
decision making, the broader the case, the greater the
power, wisdom, and chances for significant impact.
At the Washington Center in Pasadena, community
involvement literally saved the school. When the
community rallied to overcome a financial crisis, the
result was a stronger partnership and the continuation
of the optional alternative school. Whenever strong
bonds have been forged between school and community, problems have become fewer and less severe.
Reports from across the country continue to suggest
that without greater community involvement, public
education will remain a third-rate priority financially,
politically, and institutionally.

Schools Without Choice

Whether a choice is made about a traditional school
or some alternative does not matter. What matters is
that choice exists for every student, teacher, and parent
in every community. The California state legislature
in 1975 passed a bill suggesting that the public has
the right to a variety of educational modes within

public school systems to be available as needed—certainly a meaningful step toward providing, educationally, for the diversity of society. Legislation requires all schools to provide options, and therefore no California system can mandate monolithic educational programs. Once this kind of action is taken, attention can be focused on the kinds of choices best suited to each community and each individual. If the issue is forced, education will become diversified through the courts, which is not a pleasant prospect. But with the foundation well in place, choice in public education will become as important as the institution itself. Mario Fantini says it this way: "Obviously, we need a fresh plan for reform—one that brings out the best in people; one that brings the parties of interest together; one that respects the rights and responsibilities of each; one that is not imposed, does not cost more money; one that will increase satisfaction among parents, students, and teachers; one that can provide quality education to a diverse population. Fortunately, such a reform plan is emerging, which is variously being called alternative schools, alternative education, options in education, public schools of choice. Regardless of its name, the key ingredients are optional learning environments and the right of the individual choice for parents, students, and teachers."

Education Through Choice

In several thousand American communities today, families and educators have the power of choice in public education. The degree to which students, parents, and teachers select from differing school environments determines whether legitimate alternatives exist.

The diversification of education could provide structure for an educational system that would be more effective and responsive to the expectations and realities of contemporary and future societies. By virtue of choice, responsibility shifts from the school or system, which is often authoritarian, to individuals.

The concept of choice in a democracy is much more crucial than curricular content. Without choice, curriculum can become static, often irrelevant, and for many youngsters, totally unacceptable. But even more importantly, if adults in a democratic society are expected to make wise choices about important aspects of their lives, children and youth must learn to make decisions.

Because of the encouragement to share decision making in alternative schools, students experience early the need for suitable techniques and appropriate rationale for their judgments. The impact of this single aspect of the alternative school movement is overwhelming. That so few administrators are willing to allow participation in real decision making in their schools is unfortunate if not unacceptable in 1976. Naturally, participation is threatening because the power base is broadened, sometimes even weakened, and the risks become even greater. The unmistakable advantage, however, is that decision making is being learned through practice and experience.

On the basis of his experience as the director of an alternative public school, Allan Glatthorn listed these principles for decision making:

> People learn as they live. Those who live in a democracy learn to operate democratically; those who live in an autocracy learn to operate autocratically. Insofar as is possible, schools in a democracy should operate democratically.
>
> Boundaries are needed. Every community of individuals, including schools, needs limits. In a democratic community, those limits should be set by those who are part of that community.
>
> Leaders lead. Even in a democratic community, someone is in charge. It's always healthier if people are honest about the authority they possess and don't play games of participation with those who have less authority.
>
> There is no monopoly on wisdom. Problems are best

solved when all competent and informed people pool their
insights.

Students are people. Like the rest of us, they are more
likely to support and implement those decisions in which
they have had a voice.

At least 25 percent of all school-age youth drop
out of school before graduation. The importance of
choice to dropouts is obvious. If they are under the
compulsory education age, they are forced back into
the very school setting they dropped out of, and they
drop out again. If dropouts can examine alternatives,
the likelihood of their returning to school and remaining there is greatly enhanced. In Seattle, for example,
twenty-seven reentry programs attracted more than
3,000 students into the system in a single year. Students
returned largely because they could choose a school
program different from the one they had previously
dropped out of. In short, to these students, choice
can mean the difference between continuing their
formal education and accepting a situation that the
majority in society consider a mark of failure.

One promising aspect of choice as a reform strategy,
which may allow it to prevail, is perhaps best under-
stood from a historical perspective. Reform strategies,
particularly those of the 1950s and 1960s, were based
almost exclusively on imposition and excluded choice.
Basically, they were strategies developed for someone
else and by someone else without involving those who
were to be affected by the reform. These reforms failed
to produce significant changes in schools. With two
decades of educational reform efforts past, a new
transitional era, where the inception of choice could
lead to the development of a variety of different
schools, is emerging.

So far only a few systems are attempting to change
their total structure from compulsion to choice. In
Minneapolis, for example, in the fall of 1976, all
families of elementary students will have had at least
four distinctly different types of schools to choose

from. The entire Minneapolis system of public education is approaching voluntarism. As the decade ends,
it is possible that many other school systems will have
incorporated choice as the key means of making public
education responsive. No other strategy has had the
impact that potentially exists through the development
of schools of choice.

Problems and Criticisms of Decision Making

Critics of participatory decision making frequently
cite a lessened quality of judgment, an inadequate
or weakened result of decisions when the masses are
involved. In the final analysis, the will of the people
is the basis for a democratic system of government.
If weak decisions are made by the people—even on
a representative basis—the people can change the
system. Thus, to make rather rapid and sweeping
changes, people must get involved on a larger scale.
Simply identifying an unfulfilled need, perhaps by
using a community needs survey, has frequently stimulated involvement. In Tucson, the alternative school
concept was brought about largely because unfulfilled
needs within the community were expressed.

In addition, critics cite time consumption as a reason
to avoid participatory decision making. That argument
is not consistent with democratic principles, though
it may be inherently true until people learn that only
individually and collectively can they truly change,
modify, or reform anything. The optional alternative
public school movement is definitely influencing the
roles people are assuming about decision making.

A final point about decision making that often is
a stumbling block for school administrators, and for
that matter, all educators, is directly related to the
politics of accountability. The system and the people
expect the authority figure to assume responsibility.
The wise administrator, after educating the public
about whatever decision-making system is being used,
should invite them to be included in the decision-mak-

ing design. Involving the public early is a way to get support and interest on important issues.

Fear and "we've never done it that way before," along with little or no experience often get in the way of participatory decision making. Even more unfortunate, these hangups all too often become a rationale for not reforming present practices. It is a vicious circle, and until that circle is broken, as it is being broken in optional alternative public schools, decision making will continue to reflect anti-American ideals and values.

Power and Education

Authoritarian schools somehow diminish the legitimacy of a democratic society. The incongruence between a society based upon choices, freedom, liberty, opportunity, individuality, openness, and justice, and a public school system where these same elements have not existed, remains the most crucial problem facing the schools and the society they serve.

The development of optional alternative public schools has been the only significant educational movement that has attempted to align the systems of public schools with two critical elements: the relationship between schools and a democratic society, and the relationship between schools and growth, development, and learning. An abundance of literature and research indicates that a great distance lies between the public schools and knowledge of the learning and growth of children and youth. Basic to the optional alternative public schools movement is the resolution of these dilemmas and inconsistencies.

Optional alternative public schools in many parts of the country have tackled the issue of representative democracy. In St. Paul, Chicago, Madison, Los Angeles, Wichita, and other places, schools have been created by design and intent to work on democratic principles. Joint decision making, shared responsibilities throughout the school program, and built-in accountability make these schools places where students "live" rather than "prepare for life later." A "live it and learn it" philosophy permeates not only the schools but also the communities they serve.

People and Power

A struggle for power, basic and inherent in life itself, is the root of much of the conflict within society, and increasingly, in public education. An effort to make a consistent and significant change in public education relating to the role of power, authority, and governance in the optional alternative public schools is gradually beginning. Perhaps, with present efforts, a decade or two will provide ample time to lay a foundation upon which to build new and more responsive systems of public education. Nevertheless, use and misuse of power have invaded the personal lives of most Americans, and the schools must accept a sizeable responsibility for this situation.

People who do not experience power in some degree cannot be competent citizens with the moral and ethical ability to make judgments, nor will they possess the compassion needed to deal with power. By their nature, optional alternative public schools can ensure opportunities for youth to experience and learn about power and politics both individually and collectively.

Educators have been reluctant to recognize that leadership, particularly leadership leading toward change or reform, is political. The simple fact is that schools are political, and educational reform is a major political issue. Perhaps one reason educational change and reform have been so slow in coming is the lack of appropriate power or political awareness by educators. Ability to use power effectively has not been a strength of public education, though effective educational leaders tend to demonstrate characteristics not unlike those exhibited by effective politicians.

The Optimism is Real

The new era of public concern and awareness being brought about by optional alternative public schools offers educators a new challenge to assume a major leadership role. The chance to renew public education, perhaps to generate a leadership role in American life by influencing public welfare, must not be taken lightly. In this effort the optional alternative schools have a brief moment to influence public education for decades to come. If educators and the public do not accept this challenge, then humanity is the loser. The isolationism previously known so well in public education is being abandoned in favor of wider policy, operating, and governing responsibilities. The fact remains that the optional alternative school movement is here to stay, if for no other reason than that success, accomplishment, and goodwill are increasingly being shared by people who realize that education can be the basis for improving society. By 1986, if the present trend continues, optional alternative public schools will be commonplace, their rationale solid, their support substantial. The future is, indeed, in good hands. The commitment of youth to new values, to new sets of goals and different priorities, can lead only to a more significant role for education.

8

Current Developments

"The development of public schools of choice is the only major movement in American education today," Mario Fantini said in 1973. The significance of the development of alternatives in public education since 1969 has not yet been determined. Neil Postman, writing in 1971, said, "All of the reforms that will take place in education in the next decade will have their origins in the alternative school movement." Although based on subjective judgment rather than objective evidence, an opinion of many is that a new movement has been born. Philip DeTurk, headmaster of an alternative school in Pasadena, says, "The alternative school movement continues to grow in cosmic dimensions."

In chapter 2 the enrollment in alternative public schools was estimated to be about one million students or about 2 percent of the total elementary and secondary school enrollment today. Half a million more or about 1 percent may be involved in off-campus learning alternatives for school credit, excluding vocational schools and conventional work-study programs. In addition, perhaps as many as 25,000 students are enrolled in nontraditional, nonpublic schools. In other words, the number of students currently involved in alternatives is not impressive by itself. However, several related developments must be taken into consideration in assessing the significance of the movement. These include the widespread public acceptance of the alternative schools concept, national reports endorsing the development of alternative schools, the role of the alternatives in the reform and renewal of education, the relationship between alternatives and racial integration, declining test scores in the basic skills, the increase in vandalism, crime, violence, and absenteeism in the schools, and the question of the control of public education.

Widespread Public Acceptance

The 1973 Gallup Poll of Attitudes Toward Education indicated that more than 60 percent of the respondents, including 60 percent of the parents and 80 percent of the professional educators, favored the establishment of alternative public schools for "students who are not interested in, or are bored with, the usual kind of education." Coming just a few years after the media had begun to notice alternative schools (1969-70), this is a surprisingly strong endorsement. By contrast, a question in the 1975 poll on open education indicated that only 27 percent knew what "open schools" meant—more than ten years after the term had been well publicized. Barely half of those, or 13 percent, approved of open education. The 1973 question on alternative schools was not repeated in subsequent polls. One candidate for the presidency said in 1975 that if elected, he would propose an amendment to the Constitution guaranteeing every family a choice of schools.

The Ford Foundation report on alternative schools, *Matters of Choice*, in 1974 concluded, "The point has been made that alternatives are necessary and can work educationally. Whether they continue and multiply now depends more on school systems' own initiatives than on external assistance."

An alternative public school administrator in New York City, Joe Krevisky, said in the report, "The people who created this project wanted to see if this kind of thing could work in the public school system. . . . It's caught on enough so that even the most conservative kinds of people are planning alternatives in almost every high school in New York City."

In 1974 New York City was developing an optional unzoned school program in elementary, intermediate, and junior high schools "designed to give parents a choice in the kind of schooling that children will receive."

Minneapolis started the Southeast Alternatives program so that parents in one part of the city had a choice of four different types of elementary schools. This program was so well received that the Board of Education voted unanimously to extend these options to the rest of the city by 1976.

Several states have recommended the development of alternative public schools. The Illinois State Department of Education helped start several alternative schools. In 1973 the Citizens Commission on Basic Education in Pennsylvania recommended, "Educational alternatives should be encouraged within the public system as much as possible."

The California Commission for Reform of Intermediate and Secondary Education (RISE) was charged with designing "an educational system that could respond continually to changing needs in the next quarter century" to chart ways to make schools more effective, more enjoyable, and more conducive to a continued interest in learning, and to recommend immediate and long-range changes to bring about the desired results.

In 1975, the RISE Report was published, and a major recommendation was aimed at developing alternatives in education. "Learners should be able to choose from a system of multiple options in programs and learning styles" asserted the report. To meet this goal, the commission stated that school systems should provide a wide variety of options in programs and curriculum available to all learners. School systems were challenged to develop multiple instructional techniques including learning through independent study, in groups of varying size and composition, and in different locations outside school. The commission indicated that the complete range of learning options available in a school district should be carefully communicated to and discussed with each learner so intelligent decisions could be made. Two years earlier, the California Teachers Association had passed a resolution endorsing alternative public schools.

In 1975 California became the first state to mandate the establishment of alternative public schools. The Dunlap Bill, passed in June, 1975, states that any parent or guardian may request that a local school district establish an alternative school program. The bill defines alternative schools and authorizes local school districts to establish and maintain such schools.

The Fleischmann Report, produced in 1972 by the New York State Commission on the Quality, Cost, and Financing of Elementary and Secondary Education, endorsed alternative public schools, saying, "This commission believes that alternative types of public education should be available to students and parents." It also said, "It is clear that some students thrive in a conventional school system while others perform poorly, lose interest, and too frequently drop out of school. . . . To make schools more responsive to the communities they serve as well as to encourage diversity, we propose that every New York State school district begin to establish a family choice plan."

In October, 1973, the New York State Education Department published *Providing Optional Learning Environments,* which recognized a "major movement toward alternatives" and recommended the development of options in every community.

The North Central Association of Colleges and Schools in 1972 appointed a task force to formulate accreditation standards and procedures for optional schools. In 1975 three alternative public schools were approved for membership under the new *Policies and Standards for the Approval of Optional Schools and Special Function Schools.*

Educational researchers began to take an interest in alternative schools. "Society will be better off," John Pincus of the Rand Corporation wrote in 1974, "if schools could offer more diverse alternatives in respect to both organization of schools and curriculum." Christopher Jencks, author of a controversial report on inequality in education, concluded, "Our concern with making schools satisfying places for teachers and children has led us to a concern for diversity and choice."

Professional educators, particularly those who had been involved in attempts to reform the schools, were the first to see the potential in the alternative public schools. Mario Fantini, who has written extensively on public schools of choice, suggested in 1974 that alternative schools were the only way to resolve the coming power struggle between parents and teachers.

Gerald Brunetti of the University of Minnesota concluded from his observations of the Minneapolis Southeast Alternatives that the alternative public schools would survive because of "the law of expectations." Brunetti says, "Once the initial settling-in period has occurred, there exists a relatively stable school community where people basically understand the program, support it, and have expectations that it will continue to operate the way it has. Thus, the law of expectations acts as a conservative force that works, in this case, to maintain the established alternative."

Thus the final test of acceptance for each alternative school must be within its own community. In many communities the alternative schools are full and have waiting lists. Thousands of students apply each year for the few hundred openings in alternative schools in Philadelphia, Chicago, and St. Paul.

"There are very few communities in the English-speaking world where someone is not talking about starting and operating an alternative to the present publicly supported schools," Cynthia Parsons of the *Christian Science Monitor* News Service reported in

November, 1974. "And those who do the talking generally do not mean a private, independently financial institution. Instead, they mean some different kind of publicly supported school which provides a clear alternative to the other publicly supported schools in town."

National Reports Endorse Alternatives

Since 1970 at least a dozen national reports have recommended the development of optional public schools and the creation of action learning programs. The White House Conference on Children in 1970 called for "immediate, massive funding for the development of alternative optional forms of public education." The President's Commission on School Finance recommended in 1972 that alternative public schools be provided for parents and students. Four recent national reports have emphasized the need for alternatives in secondary education.

The Reform of Secondary Education

The National Commission on the Reform of Secondary Education urged in 1973 that each district should provide a broad range of alternative schools and programs, that regulations to prevent racial and socioeconomic segregation in alternatives must be established and enforced, and that mobility between alternatives should be permitted under controlled conditions.

In general, this report emphasizes the ways alternatives will complement the conventional secondary school. Although not advocating abandonment of the traditional high school, it urges recognition for a wide variety of available alternatives: "The Commission recognizes the historic and significant role the comprehensive high school has played in American education. However, it believes that the near-monopoly of secondary education by that institution, with its relatively standardized formats and restricted options, must now give way to a more diversified system of alternative schools and programs."

Two of the commission's thirty-two recommendations deal directly with alternatives. Recommendation 12, Alternative paths to high school completion, says, "Individual students must be encouraged to assume major responsibility for the determination of their educational goals, the development of the learning activities to achieve their goals, and the appraisal of their progress." The responsibility of the local school board in funding alternative programs is cited in recommendation 13: "Whenever a student chooses an acceptable alternative to the comprehensive high school, local school boards should fund his education at the level of current expenditure computed for other students."

The commission said it did not believe that the proposed system of alternative schools should cost much more than today's conventional schools. "Careful reallocation of existing resources, accompanied by reappraisal of educational priorities, should pay the bills without undue financial dislocations," the commission said. "Moving from a singular to a plural system means a shifting in the educational attitudes of everyone, from the classroom teacher to the chief school administrator." The commission also recommended awarding academic credit for accomplishments outside the building in action or experiential learning programs.

Youth: Transition to Adulthood

In 1974 the Panel on Youth of the President's Science Advisory Committee published its report *Youth: Transition to Adulthood*. This study, which grew out of concern about the ways in which young people are brought into adulthood in the United States, focuses on the relationship between schooling and the transition to adulthood. With every decade, as the labor of children has become unnecessary to society, the length of their schooling has increased. "Every society must somehow solve the problem of transforming children into adults, for its very survival depends on that solution," the report says. "In every society there is established some kind of institutional setting within which the process of transition is to occur, in directions predicated by societal goals and values. In our view, the institutional framework for maturation in the United States is now in need of serious examination."

The report seriously and constructively evaluates the appropriateness and the effectiveness of schooling in the transition to adulthood. Society has used two phases in transition so far: a work phase, in which children joined the work force as soon as their physical maturity allowed, and a schooling phase, in which youth are kept out of the labor force as long as possible. The report calls for a third phase that includes school but is neither defined by nor limited to schooling. "We are proposing the establishment of alternative environments for the transition to adulthood, environments explicitly designed to develop not only cognitive learning but other aspects of maturation as well," it states.

"Alternative Directions for Change," the fourth part of the report, recommends alternative schools, optional learning environments, and action learning programs. Rejecting a single standard, the panel says, "Diversity and plurality of paths to adulthood are important for the youth of any society." It suggests a broader array of settings for learning, both in and out of school, and proposes changes that would provide work situations for youth earlier. It recognizes that no one environment is beneficial to all youth, and that the single monolithic pattern of unbroken schooling has reduced opportunities for those who would find different paths more fruitful.

The panel also recommends a change in school structure. "American secondary education is increasingly a world of large urban districts composed of large comprehensive schools, with students assigned to schools according to the neighborhoods in which they live. We noted growing problems of this institutional arrangement: little consumer choice; the heavy weight of bureaucratic and professional controls; the large size of single-grade student strata; segregation by class, race, and ethnicity; overloading of institutional capacity by an excess of expectations and functions; and the institutional blandness that can follow from ambiguous purpose and amorphous structure."

Report of the National Panel on High Schools and Adolescent Education

In 1972 the U.S. Office of Education created a national panel to study high schools and adolescent education. The panel set out to critically analyze the high schools of the nation and suggested new directions for moving schools to better meet the problems of adolescent education. One such direction of change was the development of educational alternatives.

The panel reached four conclusions regarding the nation's high schools. First of all, in spite of the great freedom in managing local schools, the more than 16,000 different boards of education in the United States exhibit a "startling" similarity in their organization and instruction. Second, a truly comprehensive high school has rarely, if ever, been achieved, even though one of the goals of public education since the time of the Conant report in 1959 has been the comprehensive high school. A third conclusion was that big schools had a tendency to be inhumane, bureaucratic, and unsuited to individual student needs. The panel also cited evidence that the rise of the large comprehensive school had been accompanied by increased alienation of students from their peers and their environment. Finally, the panel said that schools functioned as much for custodial as for instructional purposes, concluding that schools seem to act as social "aging vats" and custodial shelters to protect the immature young, with this isolation effectively "decoupling" generations.

To correct the liabilities and problems of the isolated uniform comprehensive school, the panel made five recommendations about alternative schools, the first being that the institutions of adolescent education should attempt to create flexible and diverse environments to accommodate the innumerable differences among adolescents.

Second, some good results would likely be produced in an educational environment that combined a small enrollment with diverse offerings and much choice. Because the adolescent population is heterogeneous, the third recommendation is that a greater variety of alternatives would appeal to the broad range of students by providing more choices.

Fourth, the panel suggested several specific alternatives. One, minischools, could be set up with distinct learning situations—teacher-oriented, student-oriented, or open. "These minischools could specialize in anything from English to automobile mechanics and allow the schools to incorporate all levels of interest and ability in a productive educational system," the panel said. "Each of these minischools should be almost completely autonomous with its own staff, curriculum, and territory." Small alternative schools such as career academies, technology centers, art centers, and free schools outside the present high school would constitute a second alternative. The panel said, "In the community, these centers would broaden the horizons of both students and educators as to many learning situations available." Third, alternatives *to* schooling as well as *in* schooling should be evaluated. "Adolescents should be encouraged to investigate and participate in work experiences, community service, local government, and schools without walls," the panel said. A fourth alternative would extend to nights, weekends, and summers the availability of each school's facilities for youth and adults. Along with allowing greater flexibility, this would provide credit for new kinds of learning. To realize these four alternatives to schooling, the schools must have an open entrance-exit policy, so that students could attend school part-time, work or volunteer their services in or out of school, or attend two schools at one time.

The panel's fifth major recommendation about alternative schools encouraged the development of experiential learning outside the school, because no one institution can provide the diversity of experiences necessary to adequately meet the widely varying needs, interests, abilities, aspirations, and learning styles of adolescents. "Only the wider community, reflecting the diversities of the general population, has the flexibility and human and material resources to provide learning situations diverse in both content and style," said the panel.

The Adolescent, Other Citizens, and Their High Schools

Task Force '74, a national task force for high school reform, was established to follow up the report of the National Commission on the Reform of Secondary Education. The Task Force Report deals with three areas: citizen involvement, education for responsible citizenship, and the management of alternative schools and programs. The Task Force, recognizing in advance that its report would be disturbing to some readers, said, "The far-reaching recommendations combined in this report may suggest revolution—a quiet revolution, perhaps, but a real one. The Task Force members concluded that, unless many of the problems highlighted in this report receive high priority on our nation's work list, the vitality of our free public educational system will be in jeopardy. Though its members are not alarmists, the Task Force concluded that the democratic foundations of our country will be threatened if solutions to these problems are not found."

The report shares an enthusiasm for educational

alternatives with other reports cited. Recommendation #14 "urges school districts to move toward a system-wide range of alternatives responsive to the needs of all students."

The report gives two reasons for the failure of reform through innovations, saying, "The innovative approach was piecemeal and the effort to change the high school involved manipulating only a part of the program rather than the total process. Second, neither teachers, students, nor parents were involved sufficiently in the important decisions affecting the innovation."

The Task Force, in summarizing its report, said that certain principles would have to be accepted if educational reform in the high school was to produce a better response for all students enrolled. "These principles," the Task Force said, "revolve around the following proposals:

> Citizens and parents must become more involved in the activities of high schools.
> Students must be informed of their rights and assured that such rights will be supported by due process procedure.
> Educating for responsibility must become a primary function of the school itself.
> Alternative programs to the traditional high school must be tested and established.
> There are 15.2 million public high school students in grades 9 through 12 in America today, and among them are our future leaders. We need to do our best for them—for our sake as well as theirs."

A fifth report is being prepared by the Phi Delta Kappa Task Force on Compulsory Education and Transition for Youth. Its first recommendation is that alternative models of school and alternatives to school should be developed because schooling as it is presently organized and operated does not have a powerful, beneficial influence on student learning. The cumulative thrust of these five reports is reasonably clear: The present system of public education, particularly of the secondary school, needs major reform. The development of alternatives will be an integral part of future efforts to accomplish reform.

Alternatives in the Reform and Renewal of Education

"The most notable aspect of American education during the last two decades has been its preoccupation with change," *Saturday Review's* education editor James Cass wrote in 1973. "Reform of the schools has been the most popular game in town. Innumerable innovations have been introduced and widely accepted. . . . Vast sums of money and a good deal of creative energy have been expended. The result has sometimes been a more interesting and humane learning environment, but what happens to most children in the classroom has changed remarkably little."

For more than two decades the unsuccessful search for an educational panacea has continued. "I'm not sure we have any real clues at the present time on how to reform the educational systems," Paul Nachtigal of the Ford Foundation said in 1972. Many agree that the schools still need reform. A less widespread, but growing, realization is that few major reforms will come in this decade or this century. Christopher Jencks and Marsha Brown concluded, "Neither educators nor social scientists know how to change high schools so as to raise students' test scores, educational attainment, or occupational status." But some writers are calling for attempts to change the system, as Cass, who said, "We have no option but to seek the means for making the schools more effective for all children."

"This review has underscored the complexity of the process of organizational change in schools, our present minimal understanding of its dynamics, and the inadequacy of related theory and research," said Joseph Giacquinta in summing up research on organizational change in schools. "It is to be hoped that the simplistic explanations of the change process often found in the literature will be replaced by adequate theory to explain change and rigorous research to test the implications of the theory."

The type of research Giacquinta calls for will take decades to develop. Those who wish to see more responsive schools in this century will have to abandon the search for the panacean grail and accept more modest quests. The development of alternatives is not a panacea, but it may have the potential for the development of more responsive schools and programs.

Change cannot guarantee improvement, but no improvement can appear without it. The two major vehicles for educational change in the past two decades were instructional innovation and curricular reform. While research on the results of neither effort is encouraging, some realities related to both are often overlooked.

More than being "stylish," the innovations became a means by which the public and the profession evaluated schools: lots of innovations equaled a good school, and no innovations equaled a poor school. The innovation became a public relations tool. When a community expressed concern about some aspect of the schools, this was a good time to announce an innovation to decoy attention from the real concerns.

The curricular reforms had a facade of validity. If it was sponsored by the National Science Foundation, it must be okay. But James MacDonald says that the development of curriculum, including the reforms of the 1950s and 1960s, was primarily a historical accident.

"That alternatives in education are needed was also revealed following the curriculum 'reform' decade," Glenys Unruh said. "Overreliance on the new curricula as panaceas for the ills of education was illustrated by their low impact anywhere other than suburbia. Not only alternative types of curriculum content, methods, and materials are needed, but many other alternatives in education are possible and desirable."

Because the national reports cited previously all suggest that alternative schools should play a role in educational change, it might be appropriate to consider how the alternative school strategy differs from other change strategies.

The development of alternatives provides for a reorganization of the structure of public school systems. Unlike the curricular reforms, which were substantive, the development of alternatives does not necessarily introduce any new substance. But a change in organizational structure may be necessary as a prerequisite to other changes. Some educators believe that the bureaucratic, monolithic organizational structure of the school system makes it so resistant to change.

Choice vs. Imposition

The reform efforts of the past two decades were typically designed for everyone. The new math was for all students and all teachers. When a new curriculum is imposed on everyone, it is threatening to some, particularly to those who are convinced of the value of the former curriculum. This automatically creates resistance to the new curriculum from some teachers and parents.

Because the alternative is not for everyone, but only for the clients and staff who choose it, choice creates a commitment and a subsequent involvement by families and teachers.

Internal Intervention vs. External Intervention

Frequently the reforms of the past two decades depended upon external change agents, and often required external funds. These transient change agents were considered a temporary inconvenience by the school staff. The staff was not responsible for the change, and they assumed that after the change agent left, the school would return to normal. The directive for the innovation usually came from the central administration to the school faculty.

In contrast, the alternative tends to be a do-it-yourself operation. Control and responsibility are vested in the staff, the students, and their parents.

Action Lab vs. Model School

The model school concept assumed that once an innovation was tried, developed, and tested in one school, it could be disseminated in similar form to all schools. Again, this was part of the panacean approach. The experimental or model school rarely, if ever, produced generalizable results.

The alternative school tends to be more an action laboratory. The smaller size of most alternatives makes it possible to make more changes and to modify the changes as quickly as necessary. The advantage of the smaller school is recognized. The Ford Foundation report noted, "Small schools changed faster than large ones." Glatthorn, an alternative school administrator, points out several advantages of the small alternative school: better personal relationships, less bureaucratic control, more teacher job satisfaction, more student participation, and better personnel usage.

All of these differences suggest that renewal is more appropriate than reform for discussing the alternative schools' role in educational change. The development of alternatives is not an attempt to reform the existing institution. The conventional school will always be available, and when every family has a choice of schools, the conventional school becomes an option. Continual creation of new alternatives builds self-renewal into the system, as well.

Alternatives and Racial Integration

Several recent developments suggest that optional public schools are providing another dimension to the problem of racial segregation in the schools. In some communities the alternative schools are perceived as an alternative to compulsory busing.

In Berkeley, Evanston, Houston, Pasadena, and St.

Paul the creation of alternative public schools was part of an overall plan in each city to reduce racial imbalance in the schools. The Brown School in Louisville had an evenly divided student body, half black, half white, and waiting lists for admission, while the rest of the city and the surrounding county were in turmoil over court-ordered busing.

Legal decisions mandating busing to achieve racial balance in the schools were based in part on the research of sociologist James Coleman, though Coleman himself never recommended forced busing. "In dense and large urban areas, class integration is extremely difficult, if not impossible, to achieve," Coleman said in 1972. "What I think is needed in the long run is a new and totally different solution to what comprises a school. I would characterize this approach as a breaking apart of the school where some of the child's activities are carried out in one setting, others in another setting. Some of these activities would be class-integrated, but not all need be. When a child has a diverse array of educational settings, then it's not necessary for every one of those settings to be class-integrated."

Coleman could well have been describing the St. Paul Learning Centers Program, where students spend one-half day in their neighborhood schools, which are class segregated, and one-half day in the learning centers, which are class integrated. This voluntary integration program has attracted more than 90 percent of the eligible students. More recently, concerned about the possibility of forced busing causing "white flight" from urban areas, Coleman has suggested an open enrollment plan for metropolitan areas that would allow each student to attend any school in the area as long as the school chosen has a lower proportion of his race than the neighborhood school. This proposal would probably not affect the black inner-city school because it is doubtful that many whites would choose to attend it.

The busing controversy has attracted much attention

in all parts of the country. At least four constitutional amendments that would end forced busing have been proposed. Legislation has been introduced in Congress to reduce racial and socioeconomic segregation in the schools, including the prevention of resegregation. The National Equal Educational Opportunities Act of 1974 would establish educational parks and magnet schools available by choice and would allow voluntary transfer of students from schools in which their race is a majority to schools in which their race is a minority. Thus it seems possible, but not probable, that alternative public schools could be established by law nationally to aid integration.

Meanwhile, in at least two communities U.S. District Court judges have ruled that optional public schools had to be established as part of the resolution of segregation cases. In Detroit, Judge Robert DeMascio ruled that open enrollment schools and vocational centers would be available to all students but with controlled racial composition. In Boston, Judge W. Arthur Garrity ruled as part of a segregation case that the city would establish twenty-two magnet schools designed to draw students with "attractive and innovative programs." Judge Garrity called the magnet schools "the crux and magic" of his integration program. Attendance rates at the integrated magnet school are already higher than in the school system as a whole. Other cities using magnet schools as part of integration programs include Cleveland, Ft. Worth, and Harrisburg.

Declining Scores in the Basic Skills

People have always been concerned about how well the schools were teaching the basic skills. Since 1850 the schools have been criticized in every decade for their failure in the teaching of reading and writing. Concerns about declining scores on national tests and indications that so many American adults are both illiterate and incompetent have prompted a new wave of criticism today.

In general, the alternative schools movement has not focused on basic skills development as a major rationale, though some individual alternative schools have produced dramatic results with students who had not been achieving well in conventional schools. "Where standard measures of achievement such as test scores and college admissions are applicable, they show that alternative school students perform at least as well as their counterparts in traditional school programs, and usually better," a Ford Foundation report stated in 1974. However, few alternative schools were designed to concentrate on the basic skills. Until 1975 only about a dozen fundamental alternative public schools were operating—in California, Colorado, Florida, Maryland, Michigan, North Carolina— and their role in the alternative schools movement was slight.

However, in 1975 the Seventh Annual Gallup Poll of Public Attitudes Toward Education showed strong public interest in schools emphasizing the basic skills. Respondents were asked this question: "In some U.S. cities, parents of schoolchildren are being given the choice of sending their children to a special public school that has strict discipline, including a dress code, and that puts emphasis on the Three Rs. If you lived in one of these cities, and had children of school ages, would you send them to such a school or not?" Fifty-seven percent of total respondents and 56 percent of the parents with children in the public schools responded that they would send their children to the fundamental school.

Earlier in the same year, a panel of the National Education Association, which investigated the school textbook controversy in Kanawha County, West Virginia, recommended "that consideration be given to alternative public education emphasizing 'traditional teaching methods' within the Kanawha County public school system."

Thus, the present mood in society and in education suggests that interest in the optional fundamental public school will continue.

Vandalism, Violence, Crime, and Absenteeism

The great interest in fundamental schools is certainly related to concern with discipline as well as concern for basic skills. In the annual Gallup polls on education, lack of discipline is most frequently cited as the major problem confronting the public schools. In the 1975 poll discipline was ranked first, with busing for integration second and lack of financial support third.

Crime and vandalism in the schools cost $594 million in 1974, an amount greater than the schools spent on textbooks in the same year. Few people disagree with the report of Senator Birch Bayh's subcommittee that violence and vandalism are rapidly increasing in both intensity and frequency. Part of the increase may be due to more accurate reporting, but the 1973 report of the Commission on the Reform of Secondary Education states, "There is reason to believe that fewer than 10 percent of the crimes committed in school buildings, including violent crimes, are divulged."

Very few alternative public schools have originated as a response to absenteeism or crime. One large urban high school with a 70 percent truancy rate and a 60 percent dropout rate was converted into a complex of optional minischools in a desperate effort to save the school.

State commissions in California, New York, and Pennsylvania based part of their recommendations for creating smaller optional public schools on increases in absenteeism and crime. "The incidence of vandalism, fighting, and drug-alcohol offenses in school was directly related to size of school," according to a task force report on California schools. In *Violence in the Schools,* Michael Berger reports that the sheer size of urban schools is a cause of violence, and that there is an "almost total lack of violence in alternative schools." This is verified by reports of fewer absentees, less vandalism, and less crime from the smaller alternative public schools.

Many who are not professional educators see the alternative school as a solution to these serious problems. Both the national president of the PTA and a representative of the American Civil Liberties Union recommended alternatives to the Bayh committee investigating school violence and vandalism. A 1975 report, "Violence in Our Schools" from the National Committee for Citizens in Education, recommends alternative programs and minischools.

Alternative public schools will probably not solve the problems of absenteeism and crime in the schools, but they may have a contribution to make in the eventual diminution of these problems.

The Question of the Control of Public Education

For the past fifteen years concern about the control of the schools has been increasing. Federal and state governments have attempted to gain greater control of schools through the accountability movement, including systems development and behavioral or performance objectives. Teacher unions and associations have sought more control through contract negotiations. Parents and other citizens have tried to gain more control through the local community board and by forming national interest groups.

The development of alternative schools suggests a different control structure. Choice for students, parents, teachers, and administrators within a local school system is a direct way of getting everyone involved. Those who make choices have to be adequately prepared both to make a wise choice and to assume responsibility for the success of the alternative chosen.

Choice by the user provides a different means of control. The quality of a school system can be judged by the array and quality of alternatives it provides to its clientele. Alternatives that are not perceived as meeting an educational need will not be chosen.

Equally important, analysis of a community's need for alternatives provides a forum in which various interest groups within the community can express their educational needs and concerns. In many communities today no other means for this communication exists. A community that analyzes its needs for alternatives carefully and thoroughly and agrees that they are not necessary will have created a climate more supportive of the standard schools. Involving a broad segment of the local community in the action—the consideration of alternatives—will show all concerned that they can and do indeed have a part in the control of the local schools.

Conclusion

In the 200-year history of this country, Jefferson's ideal of an electorate educated to handle the problems of a democracy has never been farther away. Few adults today can comprehend the complexity of problems of international politics and trade, inflation and depression, the sudden emergence of a no-growth economics after two hundred years of the world's most impressive growth curve, sexual politics, environmental deterioration, inequality in economics and politics, dishonesty in business and government, and a host of other problems, present and future.

The only promising resource for the future solutions to these problems is the present generation of children and youth. At present this resource is not being developed adequately. Since elementary and secondary enrollments are not now expanding rapidly, concern for quantity of education can now switch to a concern for the quality of education. Unless the schools can change rapidly, the quality of life, as most adult Americans have experienced it, is certain to deteriorate further. Alternatives will have a role to play in the search for quality education. That role is best described in the opening paragraphs of the North Central Association's *Policies and Standards for the Approval of Optional Schools:* "In recent years the concept of educational choice (optional schools, alternative schools—call them what you will) has penetrated deeply into the American system of education. It seems likely that in the foreseeable future many different types of schools will exist side by side within the total educational structure, each designed to meet a different set of specified learning and living needs of young people. These schools will not be competitive with nor antagonistic to one another, but rather will be complementary in effort and thrust, helping American education redeem its long-term commitment to the fullest education of every child.

"While the standard school certainly will continue to be the major institution in American education, it will not be the exclusive one. Other types of schools will develop, seeking to provide more fully for the total educational needs of the community. Widespread educational options—the coexistence of many types of alternative schools and programs—should strengthen American education as a whole."

Bibliography

Books and Monographs

Bailey, Stephen, Francis Macy, and Donn Vickers. *Alternative Paths to the High School Diploma.* Reston, VA: National Association of Secondary School Principals, 1973.

Berger, Michael. *Violence in the Schools: Causes and Remedies.* Bloomington, IN: Phi Delta Kappa, 1974.

Bremer, John and Michael von Moschzisker. *The School Without Walls: Philadelphia's Parkway Program.* New York: Holt, Rinehart, and Winston, 1971.

Children's Defense Fund. *Children Out of School in America.* Cambridge, MA: Children's Defense Fund, 1974.

Cremin, Lawrence. *American Education: The Colonial Experience.* New York: Harper and Row, 1970.

Committee on the Judiciary, United States Senate, Subcommittee to Investigate Juvenile Delinquency. Birch Bayh, Chairman. *Our Nation's Schools—A Report Card: "A" in School Violence and Vandalism.* Washington, D.C.: U.S. Government Printing Office, 1975.

DeTurk, Philip. *P.S. 2001: The Story of the Pasadena Alternative School.* Bloomington, IN: Phi Delta Kappa, 1974.

Elam, Stan (ed.). *The Gallup Polls of Attitudes Toward Education, 1969-1973.* Bloomington, IN: Phi Delta Kappa, 1973.

Eurich, Alvin (ed.). *High School 1980: The Shape of the Future in American Secondary Education.* New York: Pitman, 1970.

Fantini, Mario. *Public Schools of Choice.* New York: Simon and Schuster, 1973.

_____. *What's Best for the Children?* New York: Anchor/Doubleday, 1974.

Fizzell, Robert. "Reschooling Society," doctoral dissertation, Northwestern University, 1975.

Ford Foundation. *A Foundation Goes to School.* New York: Ford, 1972.

_____. *Matters of Choice: A Ford Foundation Report on Alternative Schools.* New York: Ford, 1974.

Fritz, John. *My Encounters with Alternatives.* Toronto: Canadian Education Association, 1975.

Glatthorn, Allan. *Alternatives in Education: Schools and Programs.* New York: Dodd, Meade, 1975.

Goodlad, John et. al. *The Conventional and the Alternative in Education.* Berkeley: McCutchan, 1975.

157

Hunt, David and Edmund Sullivan. *Between Psychology and Education.*
   Hinsdale, IL: Dryden, 1974.
Hunt, David. *Matching Models in Education.* Toronto: Ontario Institute
   for Studies in Education, 1971.
Institute for the Development of Educational Activities. *Developing
   New Models, Methods, and Means for Education.* Dayton: IDEA,
   1974.
Martin, John and Charles Harrison. *Free to Learn: Unlocking and
   Ungrading American Education.* Englewood Cliffs: Prentice-Hall,
   1972.
National Commission on the Reform of Secondary Education. B. Frank
   Brown, Chairman. *The Reform of Secondary Education.* New York:
   McGraw-Hill, 1973.
National Commission on Resources for Youth. *New Roles for Youth
   in the School and the Community.* New York: Citation, 1974.
National Committee for Citizens in Education. *Violence in Our Schools.*
   Columbia, MD: National Committee for Citizens in Education, 1975.
National Association of Secondary School Principals. *American Youth
   in the Mid-Seventies.* Reston, VA: National Association of Secondary
   School Principals, 1973.
_____. *The Mood of American Youth.* Reston, VA: National Association
   of Secondary School Principals, 1974.
*National Panel on High Schools and Adolescent Education (Report of
   The)* of the U.S. Office of Education (prepublication discussion draft).
   John Henry Martin, Chairman. 1974.
North Central Association of Colleges and Schools. *Policies and Stan-
   dards for the Approval of Optional Schools and Special Function
   Schools.* Chicago: North Central Association, 1974.
Panel on Youth of the President's Science Advisory Committee. James
   S. Coleman, Chairman. *Youth: Transition to Adulthood.* Chicago:
   University of Chicago Press, 1974.
Riordan, Robert. *Alternative Schools in Action.* Bloomington, IN: Phi
   Delta Kappa, 1972.
Sarason, Seymour. *The Culture of the School and the Problem of Change.*
   Boston: Allyn and Bacon, 1971.
Scribner, Harvey and Leonard Stevens. *Make Your Schools Work.* New
   York: Simon and Schuster, 1975.
Sherman, Stanley, David Zuckerman, and Alan Sostek. *The Anti-
   achiever: Rebel Without a Future.* Boston: The University Center,
   1972.
Sizer, Theodore. *Places for Learning, Places for Joy.* Cambridge: Harvard
   University Press, 1973.
Task Force on Compulsory Education and Transition for Youth of Phi
   Delta Kappa (prepublication draft). Maurice Gibbons, Chairman.
   Education for the Transition to Adulthood: A Proposal.
Task Force on Secondary Schools in a Changing Society of the National

Association of Secondary School Principals. *Secondary Schools in a Changing Society: This We Believe.* Reston, VA: National Association of Secondary School Principals, 1975.

Task Force '74, A National Task Force for High School Reform. B. Frank Brown, Director. *The Adolescent, Other Citizens, and Their High Schools.* New York: McGraw-Hill, 1975.

Toffler, Alvin (ed.). *Learning for Tomorrow: The Role of the Future in Education.* New York: Random House, 1974.

Weinstock, Ruth. *The Greening of the High School.* New York: Educational Facilities Laboratories, 1973.

Yankelovich, Daniel. *The New Morality: A Profile of American Youth in the '70s.* New York: McGraw-Hill, 1974.

Articles and Chapters

Bane, Mary Jo and Christopher Jencks, "The Schools and Equal Opportunity," *Saturday Review,* September 16, 1972, pp. 37-42.

Brunetti, Gerald, "Alternative Schools: Can They Survive?" *The Clearing House,* 48:5, January, 1974, pp. 267-271.

Coleman, James, "How Do The Young Become Adults?" in *Changing Education: Alternatives From Educational Research.* Englewood Cliffs: Prentice-Hall, 1973, pp. 169-178.

Duffy, E. J., "Directions for Learning—We Have The Tools," in *The '80s: Where Will The Schools Be?* Reston, VA: National Association of Secondary School Principals, 1974, pp. 4-8.

Gallup, George, "Seventh Annual Gallup Poll of Public Attitudes Toward Education," *Phi Delta Kappan,* 57:4, December, 1975, pp. 227-241.

Giacquinta, Joseph, "The Process of Organizational Change in Schools," in *Review of Research in Education,* Volume 1. Itasca, IL: Peacock, 1973, pp. 178-208.

Gibbons, Maurice, "The Australian Walkabout: A Model for Transition to Adulthood," *Phi Delta Kappan,* 55:9, May, 1974, pp. 596-602.

Glatthorn, Allan, "Decision Making in Alternative Schools," *NASSP Bulletin,* 57:374, September, 1973, pp. 110-119.

Hunt, David, "Person-Environment Interaction: A Challenge Found Wanting Before It Was Tried," *Review of Educational Research,* 45:2, Spring, 1975, pp. 209-230.

Jencks, Christopher and Marsha Brown, "Effects of High Schools on Their Students," *Harvard Educational Review,* 45:3, August, 1975, pp. 273-324.

Joyce, Bruce, "Curriculum and Humanistic Education: 'Monolism' vs. 'Pluralism,'" in *Radical School Reform.* Boston: Little, Brown, 1973, pp. 250-271.

Paskal, Dolores and William Miller, "Managing Controversy About Optional and Alternative Programs," *Educational Leadership,* 33:1, October, 1975, pp. 14-16.

Passow, Harry, "Reforming America's High Schools," *Phi Delta Kappan*, 56:9, May, 1975, pp. 587–590.

Sperry, Roger, "Left-Brain, Right-Brain," *Saturday Review*, August 9, 1975, pp. 30–33.

Index